JO IPPOLITO CHRISTENSEN, a former instructor at the University of Alaska, is the author of several other books, including three published by Spectrum Books/Prentice-Hall: *The Needlepoint Book, Teach Yourself Needlepoint,* and *Needlepoint: The Third Dimension.*

## BOOKS IN THE CREATIVE HANDCRAFTS SERIES:

THE CREATIVE HANDCRAFT SERIES

A SPECTRUM BOOK  PRENTICE-HALL, INC. Englewood Cliffs, N.J. 07632

# THE 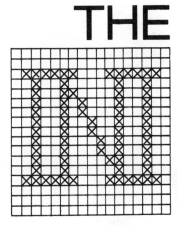EEDLEPOINT SCRAPS BOOK

What to Do With Your Needlepoint Leftovers

## Jo Ippolito Christensen

*Library of Congress Cataloging in Publication Data*

Christensen, Jo Ippolito.
    The needlepoint scraps book.

    "A Spectrum Book."
    Includes index.
    1. Canvas embroidery.  I. Title.
TT778.C3C479        746.2′24        81-17936
                                    AACR2

ISBN 0-13-611012-6 {PBK}

ISBN 0-13-611020-7

This Spectrum Book is available to businesses and organizations at a special discount when ordered in large quantities. For information, contact Prentice-Hall, Inc., General Book Division, Special Sales, Englewood Cliffs, N.J. 07632.

10  9  8  7  6  5  4  3  2  1

Printed in the United States of America

Editorial/production supervision by *Cyndy Lyle Rymer*
Page layout by *Diane Heckler-Koromhas*
Manufacturing buyer: *Cathie Lenard*

Prentice-Hall International, Inc., *London*
Prentice-Hall of Australia Pty. Limited, *Sydney*
Prentice-Hall of Canada, Ltd., *Toronto*
Prentice-Hall of India Private Limited, *New Delhi*
Prentice-Hall of Japan, Inc., *Tokyo*
Prentice-Hall of Southeast Asia Pte. Ltd., *Singapore*
Whitehall Books Limited, *Wellington, New Zealand*

This book is dedicated to my editor and friend, Lynne Lumsden. Her professionalism, her patience, and her sound advice have been invaluable to me.

# CONTENTS

# PREFACE

In these times of inflation and an uncertain economy, we are all concerned with making our dollars go farther. In needlepoint, we can best do this by keeping ourselves busy with the supplies we already have on hand. With a little work, a little imagination, and expert finishing, we can truly make something out of nothing.

If you are new to needlepoint, this is the book for you. The projects call for small quantities of yarn and/or canvas. So, with only a little outlay of cash, you can give needlepoint a try.

Part I teaches you what you need to know about needlepoint supplies and techniques.

Part II contains nineteen projects. Some of these projects employ just about any color yarn you might happen to have on hand. Others may call for, say, blues and greens, but there is great leeway in their selections. All of the projects are illustrated with black-and-white photos and line drawings, some with a color photo, and they are further explained by a text that guides you through their construction. The level of expertise varies from early to advanced.

Chapter 3 explains how to work seven small items that can be worked with scraps of yarn as well as canvas.

Chapter 4 outlines four projects that call for only scraps of yarn for the design. The background yarn, however, is not necessarily something you may have on hand; you may also need to buy canvas of an appropriate size.

Chapter 5 shows you how to make eight projects that use scraps of yarn for both the design and the background. The canvas may not necessarily be a scrap.

Part III contains all of the stitches that you will need to make the projects in this book. The diagrams are clear, but be sure to read "How to Read the Diagrams" on page 88. Photographs show you what these stitches look like when the diagram is translated into yarn. Handy charts give you the characteristics of each of these stitches.

Finally, Part IV teaches you how to block and finish the projects you have just learned how to make.

Let your imagination go wild! Have fun!


*Jo Christensen*

# ACKNOWLEDGMENTS

These few words of thanks are hardly adequate for expressing my deep appreciation of the numerous hours many people have given to this book.

Stevie Breland has worked very hard to produce the art work shown in this book. Her drawings are neat, professional, and easy to read.

Many of Jim Long's photos are reprinted from my book *The Needlepoint Book* (Prentice-Hall). Jim Keeney took the rest. Without them, all of this would be Greek! Thanks to both Jims for a super job.

Many of my friends and students have nicely allowed me to photograph and explain to you how to make their wonderful projects: Jackie Beaty (Tunic and Sampler Pillow), Barbara Johnston (Flower Eyeglass Cases), Willard Lockett (Vase of Flowers), Marlene Meek (Country Kitchen), Mary Savage (Mouse and Cheese), and Diana Smith (Computer

Tote Bag). I wish to offer a special thanks to the late Mickey McKitrick for her Basket of Strawberries. Murray Baxter built the beautiful Crayon Box and the exquisite Jewelry Box.

Jo Anne Keeney, a college English teacher, proofread my sloppy handwritten manuscript and picked on awkward phrases, bad transitions, and commas (too many and too few)!

Sharon Homer, my secretary, did a terrific job at typing stacks of letters, and Peggy George graciously typed the manuscript after Sharon moved away.

Lynne Lumsden, my editor, is great! She serves as editor, friend, and mother hen. I couldn't do it without her.

Thanks also goes to Cyndy Lyle Rymer, production editor for this book, and to Diane Heckler-Koromhas, who did the page layout.

# PART ONE
# SUPPLIES & BASIC PROCEDURES

Needlepoint is fun to do—and it's relaxing, too. You can be imaginative as well as creative. If you've done any needlepoint at all, you have scraps of yarn and canvas, as I do. The purpose of this book is to find ways to turn your scraps (and mine) into attractive and useful projects. You don't need to be an expert to benefit from this book. The projects range from easy to challenging.

# Chapter one

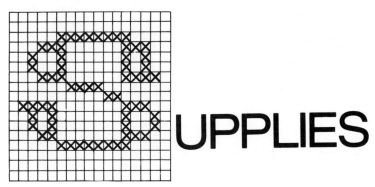

# UPPLIES

Because all the projects in this book use blank canvas (or prefinished needlepoint pieces) and yarn, I'm going to discuss only those supplies and techniques needed to do this kind of needlepoint.

If you don't have any scraps, don't despair. Yarn can be bought in small quantities, and many needlework shops sell canvas by the square inch and would be glad to cut any size you need. If they won't, another project in the book will use the scraps you've just acquired from making one project.

## Canvas

Needlepoint is stitched on a background fabric called canvas. The threads are woven rather far apart and are called *mesh.* This creates holes through which yarn, threaded on a blunt-tipped needle, is passed.

The quality of the canvas you buy is important. Your time and effort would be wasted on an inferior quality canvas that would come apart in finishing or during use. Flaws can also keep your stitches from being even. Any reputable shopowner will gladly cut around them.

There are basically two kinds of canvas—Penelope and Mono.

## Penelope canvas

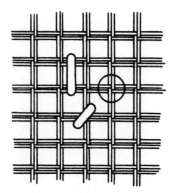

**Fig. 1-1** *Penelope canvas (junction of mesh circled)*

When the canvas threads are woven in pairs, the canvas is identified as *Penelope* canvas. Each pair of threads is considered one *mesh* (see Figure 1–1). Notice that one pair of threads runs more closely together than the other pair. This closely woven pair should always run vertically. Your eyes may have a hard time seeing the difference at first, but eventually you will be able to see the difference. Penelope canvas is strong.

## Mono canvas

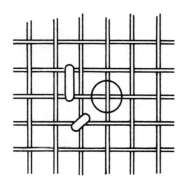

**Fig. 1-2** *Regular Mono canvas (junction of mesh circled)*

Mono canvas is woven so that each thread is a single mesh. There are two kinds of Mono canvas—Regular and Interlock.

**REGULAR MONO CANVAS**  The threads are woven over, under, over, under, and so on in a loose fashion (see Figure 1–2). The junction of the mesh is held together only by sizing. As you work on this canvas, the sizing softens and the mesh move. This can be a nuisance in working many stitches. However, this property makes Regular Mono canvas ideal for chair seats and other upholstered items, especially when it is stitched in Basketweave, which is also flexible. Do check the stitch instructions for working Basketweave on Regular Mono canvas (see page 104). Many stitches cannot be worked on this canvas, or need special instruction. Be sure to read "How to Read the Diagrams" (see page 88), which will help

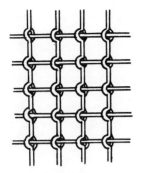

**Fig. 1-3** *Interlock Mono canvas*

you to identify these stitches. Stitching on a frame helps a great deal in keeping this canvas in shape.

**INTERLOCK CANVAS**   The junctions of the mesh are secured on Interlock Canvas, sometimes called Leno (see Figure 1–3). A separate thread is twisted around the mesh to lock these junctions. This canvas does not ravel easily. This canvas *must* be used any time a shape other than a square or rectangle is needed.

The following list gives the pros and cons of Regular and Interlock canvas.

## Regular Mono Canvas

| PRO | CON |
|---|---|
| • Round thread; covers better. | • Stitch tensions cause it to distort more easily. |
| • Soft; good for pulled thread. | • Softness causes distortion more easily. |
| • Basketweave has even more give than on other canvases. | • *Must* stitch on a frame. |
| • Needed for applique. | • Hard for beginners to learn on. |

## Interlock Mono Canvas

| PRO | CON |
|---|---|
| • Helps you to maintain even stitch tension, which is invaluable for beginners. | • Harsh, but it softens as you stitch. |
| | • Harshness shreds yarn; you must stitch with shorter yarn. |
| • Finishing is easier because it does not ravel easily. | • Cannot use for applique. |

## Canvas mesh count and stitch size

In discussing canvas, the words *Penelope* and *Mono* are followed by numbers. These numbers indicate how many mesh there are per linear inch. Unfortunately, this number is not accurate over a large area. So if you need a particular number of mesh, count them out; don't measure by the inch.

Penelope canvas comes in 3½, 4, 5, 7, and 10. Mono is available in 4, 5, 7, 8, 10, 12, 13, 14, 16, 18, 20, 22, and 24. Penelope 10 is the most versatile canvas. Cross Stitches do best on Penelope or Mono 7 or 8. Straight Stitches do best on Mono 14 (Figure 1–4 a–e shows several of these canvases).

**Fig. 1-4a** *Penelope 4 worked with rug yarn*

**Fig. 1-4b** *Penelope 7 worked with rug yarn*

**Fig. 1-4c** *Penelope 10 worked with Persian yarn*

**Fig. 1-4d** *Interlock Mono 14 worked with Persian yarn*

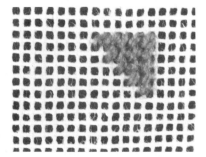

**Fig. 1-4e** *Regular Mono 18 worked with Persian yarn*

## Plastic canvas

Plastic canvas makes finishing extremely easy. It does not ravel. Also, it comes in just a few mesh sizes. It can be bought by the yard, by the sheet, and in various shapes, such as squares, circles, diamonds, and hexagons (see Figure 1–5).

**Fig. 1-5** *3 inch plastic square (7 mesh per inch)*

## Breakaway (waste) canvas

**Fig. 1-6**

Beware of Breakaway (waste) canvas (see Figure 1–6). It is made for stitching Cross Stitches onto fabric. When the canvas is wet, the sizing dissolves. The mesh are then *very* weak. *DO NOT* use it for needlepoint.

# Needles

Needlepoint is stitched with a blunt-end tapestry needle (see Figure 1–7). The needle should pass easily through the holes of the canvas, yet the eye must be big enough to hold yarn

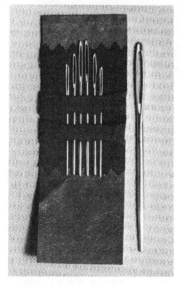

that is fat enough to cover the canvas. The threaded needle should not distort the hole of the canvas as it passes through. Use the following chart to help select the right size needle for your canvas.

| CANVAS SIZE | NEEDLE SIZE |
|:---:|:---:|
| 3–5 | 13 |
| 7–8 | 16 |
| 10 | 18–20 |
| 12–14 | 20 |
| 16–20 | 22 |
| 22–24 | 24 |

**Fig. 1-7** *Blunt-end tapestry needles: Sizes 22, 20, 18, 18, 20, 22, 13 (from left to right)*

## Threading the needle

Lots of people think that threading the needle is the hardest part of needlepoint. But it doesn't have to be.

Figure 1–8, a–b shows the paper method. It always works, but the hard part is keeping up with the little piece of paper!

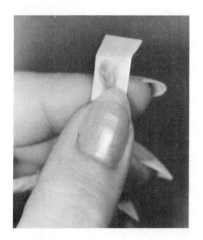

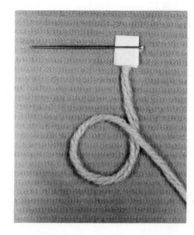

**Fig. 1-8 a & b**
*Threading the needle: The paper method*

The loop method is reliable (see Figure 1–9, a–c). Fold the yarn over the tip of the needle. Squeeze your thumbnail against the needle and then push the loop through the eye.

Many of my students like a metal needle threader. If you want to try that, keep it handy by tying it to the margin of your canvas with a piece of yarn.

There are times when no method seems to work. Try turning the needle over and attacking the eye from the other side. The hole seems to be bigger on one side than the other. But those who know about such things say that's impossible. Nevertheless, it works!

If that doesn't work, try threading the other end of the yarn. Threading the needle against the nap of the yarn is hard (see Yarn nap, page 23).

(a)

(b)

(c)

**Fig. 1-9 a-c** *Threading the needle: The loop method*

# Yarn

There are many kinds of yarn that can be used for needle-point. However, better-looking and longer-wearing projects can be created by stitching with yarn made especially for needlepoint. The canvas is harsh, and it wears yarn thin. Needlepoint yarn is made with long, strong fibers so that it can stand up against the canvas. It is also mothproofed.

Most yarn (including needlepoint yarn) comes in dye lots. The color can vary from one vat of dye to the next. Therefore, you need to buy all the yarn for your project at one time. Once in a while we all miscalculate. In that case, blend in a new dye lot shade by following the directions on shading.

There are two kinds of needlepoint yarn: tapestry yarn and Persian yarn.

**TAPESTRY YARN**  Tapestry yarn (see Figure 1–10a) looks like knitting worsted. It is a tightly twisted four-ply strand of wool yarn. This tight twist makes a smooth, pretty and long-wearing stitch. This same tight twist, however, makes separating the plies difficult. Thus, thickening or thinning this type of yarn is very difficult. Shading is better accomplished with Persian yarn. Tapestry yarn is generally packaged in 100, 40, 12.5, 10, and 8.8 yard skeins.

**PERSIAN YARN**  Persian yarn (see Figure 1–10b) is a loosely twisted three-ply yarn. Each of these three plies is a two-ply strand that is not meant to be separated. Actually, Persian yarn is six-ply, but for some strange reason it is called

**Fig. 1-10a**  *Four-ply tapestry yarn*     **Fig. 1-10b**  *Three-ply Persian yarn*

three-ply in this country. The three plies are easily separated so that thickening, thinning, and shading can be readily accomplished. Persian yarn comes in many marvelous colors with great ranges of shades in one family. They're great for Bargello patterns (see page 89). You can buy Persian yarn by the strand (approximately 66" long), by the ounce, by the pound, and in various sized skeins. There is a great range in quality among Persian yarns. Price is usually a good guideline. You still get what you pay for.

**NOVELTY YARNS** Novelty yarns dress up a needlepoint piece. They add shimmer, texture, and interest. You've got to be careful with them, however. They are not as strong as wool needlepoint yarns, and, thus, they fray easily. Use a very short strand (see "Handling the Yarn," page 23). Do not use novelty yarns on items that will get lots of wear. The yarns are too fragile to stand hard use. Projects in this book use the following novelty yarns: embroidery floss (see Figure 1–10c), metallic yarn (see Figure 1–10d), velvet or velour (see Figure 1–10e), pearl cotton (see Figure 1–10f), four-ply rayon floss (see Figure 1–10g), and linen thread.

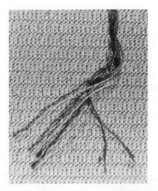

**Fig. 1-10c** *Six-ply embroidery floss*

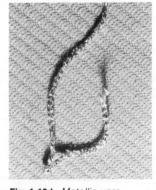

**Fig. 1-10d** *Metallic yarn*

**Fig. 1-10e** Velvet or Velour yarn

**Fig. 1-10f** Pearl Cotton

**Fig. 1-10g** *Four-ply rayon floss*

**HOW MUCH YARN TO BUY** Ideally, to figure out how much yarn to buy, you should work one square inch of the stitch you wish to use, in the brand and color of yarn you wish to use, on the canvas you will use. By keeping track of the amount of yarn it took and multiplying by the number of square inches in your design, you can figure out how much yarn you will need.

Not easy, you say? True. But the following charts will help you figure out how much yarn is needed for the stitches used in this book. Because there are so many variables, these charts are not absolutely accurate. The amounts of yarn indicated for any stitch can be used on Penelope canvas or on Mono 10, 12, or 14 canvases. (There is only a 5 percent difference in the amounts of yarn needed for 10 and 14 canvas.) Ripping was *not* allowed for. (Remember that you cannot reuse yarn that has been ripped out.) I did allow a 5 percent fudge factor to compensate somewhat for some of the variables. All inches and centimeters were generally rounded to the next highest whole number, ounces and grams to four decimal places, and yards to the nearest $1/16$ of a yard. All measurements are for three-ply Persian yarn. When more or less than three-ply was used, adjustments have already been made.

To find any of the stitches listed, please consult the index.

**EASY PROJECT PLANNER** "Now," you say, "that's well and good to know how much yarn I need per square inch, but it doesn't do me any good if I don't know how many square inches there are in my design!" True—but my Easy Project Planner will solve this problem (see Figure 1–11). It is an acrylic sheet with a grid of square inches or centimeters. When it is laid over your design, you can count the number of square inches in each color. Estimate portions of one square inch and add together halves, thirds, or quarters of square inches.

To make the Easy Project Planner, buy two $1/16''$ thick sheets of acrylic or Plexiglas from a shop that sells glass. Mine is 18″ × 18″ and I think it's a handy size. However, if scraps of another size are available to you, by all means consider using two of that size.

From an engineering supply house, purchase black tape $1/32''$ wide. You will need 684 inches, or 19 yards, of tape to make an 18″ × 18″ Easy Project Planner ruled in square inches, and 1,692 inches, or 47 yards, of tape for the same

**Fig. 1-11** *Using the Easy Project Planner*

size ruled in square centimeters. While you're at the engineering supply house, also buy a sheet of graph paper at least 18″ × 18″ with square inches (or square centimeters) marked off in dark lines.

To put the lines on the Plexiglas, tape the graph paper to a table. Place the Plexiglas on top of it. Line up the edges with the graph paper grid as well as you can. Lay the tape on the Plexiglas, using the graph paper grid as a guide (see Figure 1–12). Put another sheet of Plexiglas on top of the first so that the tape is sandwiched between them. Bind the edges with duct tape.

There are many uses for your Easy Project Planner besides figuring square inches. For example, you can use it to enlarge or reduce a drawing. It can help you to draw an item from real life (such as a vase of flowers) even if you cannot draw (see Figure 1–13). Have a groove sawed in a 4″ × 4″ piece of wood for a stand. The groove should be 2¾″ to 3″ deep and just wide enough for the Easy Project Planner to fit in it. Set it before the object(s) you wish to draw. On a blank sheet of paper, draw a grid. A one-inch grid will reproduce the object the same size as you see it through the Easy Project Planner. A smaller grid on your blank paper will reduce it, and a larger one will enlarge it.

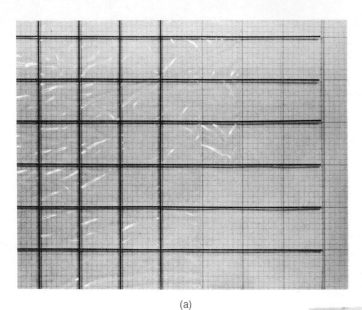

(a)

**Fig. 1-12 a & b** *Lay black tape 1/32" wide over the lines on the graph paper, which is underneath a sheet of acrylic.*

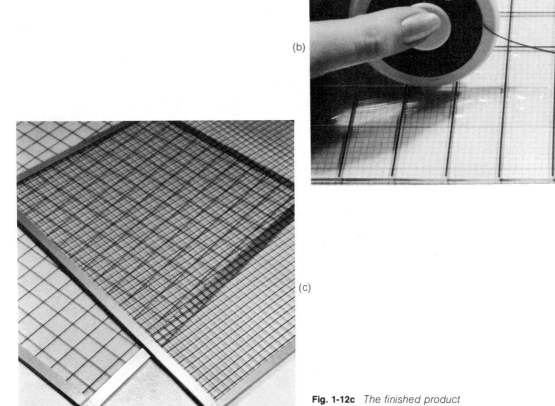

(b)

(c)

**Fig. 1-12c** *The finished product*

**Fig. 1-13a** *Slide the Easy Project Planner into a wooden stand.*

**Fig. 1-13b** *Draw the lines inside each square. This is the first rough drawing. Polish it for a design ready to stitch.*

# Other equipment

Compared to other hobbies, needlepoint doesn't require much in the way of equipment. However, what you do use should be of good quality (see Figure 1–14).

You will need two pair of scissors—a pair of fine-pointed, sharp embroidery scissors for ripping (sorry about that!) and a pair of large, crummy ones to cut canvas (canvas dulls scissors quickly). Tweezers make ripping easier (see "Ripping," page 33). You'll also need good masking tape to bind the raw edges of the canvas. (The cheap stuff just doesn't stick well.) Adhesive and freezer tape work well, too.

A ruler or yardstick is needed to measure the canvas. A crochet hook is handy in burying short tails of yarn. A thimble is not necessary, but if you're used to using one, you'll want it.

Use a *waterproof* marker or acrylic paint to draw on the canvas. Always test the marker (or paint)—*never* take the manufacturer's word that it is waterproof. Mark on a scrap of canvas. Let it dry completely—overnight if you can. Put the canvas under running water. Blot with a white tissue. If you can see color, do not use that marker or paint on that brand of

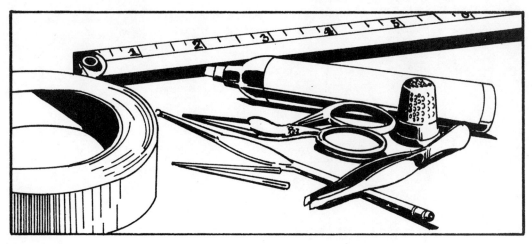

**Fig. 1-14** *Equipment needed for needlepoint*

canvas. Don't throw it away—it may work on another brand of canvas. Always test each brand of marker on each brand of canvas *yourself*. Often a marker is permanent on surfaces other than canvas. Beware.

A frame (see Figure 1–15a) is essential to even stitches and to minimal distortion of canvas. The scroll, or rotating, frame allows you to keep just the portion where you are stitching before you. The rest of your work is kept clean and rolled up.

To use this frame, sew your canvas to the twill tape before you start to stitch (see Figure 1–15b). Put the raw edge of the canvas under the tape. This keeps yarn from catching on the rough edge as well as preventing raveling. Fix the frame so the wing nuts are on the top of the frame. If they're on the bottom, they will snag your clothes.

Roll the canvas up so that the portion you are stitching on is taut. Keep it this way as long as you stitch. When you put your work away, loosen the canvas slightly. A scroll frame cannot be used with textured stitches. If you do, they will be crushed.

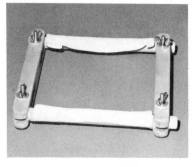

**Fig. 1-15a** *Scroll frame*

*SUPPLIES & BASIC PROCEDURES*

**Fig. 1-15b** *Attach canvas to twill tape by sewing.*

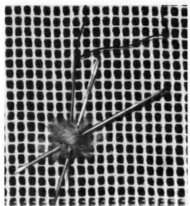

**Fig. 1-15c** *Stitch a Double Leviathan stitch to park the needles.*

| NAME OF STITICH | Number of Ply used | Inches of Yarn/sq. in. | Yards of Yarn/sq. in. | Ounces of Yarn/sq. in. | Centimeters of Yarn/sq. cm. | Grams of Yarn/sq. cm. |
|---|---|---|---|---|---|---|
| Basketweave | 3 | 45 | 1¼ | .0286 | 18 | .1255 |
| Binding Stitch | 3 | 20* | $^9/_{16}$* | .0127* | 8** | .0558** |
| Brick | 3 | 27 | ¾ | .0171 | 11 | .0753 |
| Byzantine #1 | 3 | 35 | 1 | .0222 | 14 | .0976 |
| Cashmere | 3 | 37 | 1 | .0235 | 15 | .1032 |

* per linear inch
**per linear centimeter

| NAME OF STITCH | Number of Ply used | Inches of Yarn/sq. in. | Yards of Yarn/sq. in. | Ounces of Yarn/sq. in. | Centimeters of Yarn/sq. cm. | Grams of Yarn/sq. cm. |
|---|---|---|---|---|---|---|
| Chain | 3 | 32 | 7/8 | .0203 | 13 | .0893 |
| Continental | 3 | 45 | 1¼ | .0286 | 18 | .1255 |
| Couching | 4 | 22 | 2/3 | .0140 | 9 | .0614 |
| Cross | 2 | 36 | 1 | .0229 | 14 | .1004 |
| Cut Turkey Work | 3 | 90 | 2½ | .0571 | 35 | .2511 |
| Diagonal Cashmere | 3 | 33 | 7/8 | .0210 | 13 | .0921 |
| Diagonal Hungarian Ground | 3 | 35 | 1 | .0222 | 14 | .0976 |
| Diagonal Mosaic | 3 | 36 | 1 | .0229 | 14 | .1004 |
| Double Brick | 4 | 34 | 1 | .0216 | 14 | .0949 |
| Double Stitch | 2 | 34 | 1 | .0216 | 13 | .0949 |
| Fern | 3 | 42 | 1⅛ | .0267 | 17 | .1172 |
| French Knot | 3 | 74 | 2 | .0470 | 29 | .2065 |
| Giant Brick | 4 | 36 | 1 | .0229 | 14 | .1004 |
| Giant Rice | 3 | 32 | 7/8 | .0203 | 12 | .0893 |
| Greek | 2 | 22 | 5/8 | .0140 | 9 | .0614 |
| Half Cross | 3 | 29 | 7/8 | .0184 | 11 | .0809 |
| Hitched Cross | 3 | 35 | 1 | .0222 | 14 | .0976 |
| Horizontal Brick | 4 | 36 | 1 | .0229 | 14 | .1004 |
| Horizontal Milanese | 4 | 38 | 1 1/16 | .0241 | 15 | .1060 |
| Horizontal Old Florentine | 4 | 38 | 1 1/16 | .0241 | 15 | .1060 |
| Hungarian | 3 | 27 | ¾ | .0171 | 11 | .0753 |
| Irregular Continental | 3 | 38 | 1 1/16 | .0241 | 15 | .1060 |
| Jacquard | 3 | 42 | 1⅛ | .0267 | 16 | .1172 |
| Lazy Kalem | 3 | 45 | 1¼ | .0286 | 18 | .1255 |
| Long Upright Cross | 3 | 35 | 1 | .0222 | 14 | .0976 |

| NAME OF STITCH | Number of Ply used | Inches of Yarn/sq. in. | Yards of Yarn/sq. in. | Ounces of Yarn/sq. in. | Centimeters of Yarn/sq. cm. | Grams of Yarn/sq. cm. |
|---|---|---|---|---|---|---|
| Looped Turkey Work | 3 | 90 | 2½ | .0571 | 35 | .2511 |
| Milanese | 3 | 57 | 1⅝ | .0362 | 22 | .1590 |
| Moorish | 3 | 36 | 1 | .0229 | 14 | .1004 |
| Mosaic | 3 | 38 | 1¹/₁₆ | .0241 | 15 | .1060 |
| Needleweaving | 3 | 35 | 1 | .0222 | 14 | .0976 |
| Oblong Cross | 2 | 36 | 1 | .0229 | 14 | .1004 |
| 1 × 1 Spaced Cross Tramé | 2 | 38 | 1¹/₁₆ | .0241 | 15 | .1060 |
| 1 × 3 Spaced Cross Tramé | 2 | 21 | ⅝ | .0133 | 8½ | .0586 |
| Oriental | 3 | 41 | 1⅛ | .0260 | 16 | .1144 |
| Parisian | 3 | 26 | ¾ | .0165 | 10 | .0725 |
| Pavillion | 3 | 24 | ⅔ | .0152 | 9 | .0670 |
| Reversed Mosaic | 3 | 38 | 1¹/₁₆ | .0241 | 15 | .1060 |
| Reversed Scotch | 3 | 39 | 1¹/₁₆ | .0248 | 15 | .1088 |
| Reversed Smyrna Cross | 2 | 39 | 1¹/₁₆ | .0248 | 15 | .1088 |
| Ridged Spider Web | 3 | 83 | 2⅓ | .0527 | 33 | .2316 |
| Ringed Daisies | 2 | 39 | 1¹/₁₆ | .0248 | 15 | .1088 |
| Running Stitch | 3 | 15 | ½ | .0095 | 6 | .0418 |
| Scotch | 3 | 39 | 1¹/₁₆ | .0248 | 15 | .1088 |
| Slanted Gobelin | 3 | 26 | ¾ | .0165 | 10 | .0725 |
| Smyrna Cross | 2 | 39 | 1¹/₁₆ | .0248 | 15 | .1088 |
| Straight Gobelin | 4 | 35 | 1 | .0222 | 14 | .0976 |
| Straight Stitch | 3 | 30 | ⅞ | .0190 | 12 | .0837 |
| Twisted Chain | 3 | 43 | 1¼ | .0273 | 17 | .1200 |
| Upright Cross | 2 | 32 | ⅞ | .0203 | 12 | .0893 |
| Web | 2 | 38 | 1¹/₁₆ | .0241 | 15 | .1060 |

Chapter two

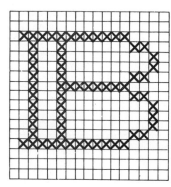

# ASIC
# PROCEDURES

Needlepoint is fun! Following some rules will help you to improve the quality of your work. But for some of you, following rules is a drag—so forget them. Be comfortable with needlepoint and do what you want. But for those of you who want some hints, here they are.

## Keeping yarn

Soda pop or beer can holders make a neat organizer for yarn, particularly if you're working with close shades of one color (see Figure 2–1a–b). An embroidery hoop also does the job. Figure 2–2a–d shows you how to knot the yarn for storage. This keeps it free from tangles. To untie, simply pull the ends.

Always keep track of the color name or number. This makes it easier to buy more just like it. Tape a bit of the yarn to the label.

**Fig. 2-1a** *Loop yarn for your current project on a plastic holder for soda pop beer cans.*

**Fig. 2-1b** *Remove one strand at a time easily.*

(a)

(b)

(c)

**Fig. 2-2a-d** *Knotting yarn for storage.*

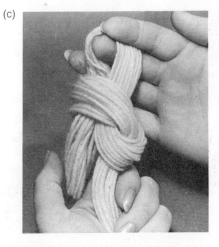

*Basic Procedures*

**21**

There are a few things you need to do before you stitch. First, measure the canvas carefully before you cut. Make sure it's big enough. Always allow a 2″ margin all the way around your design. This makes finishing easier. Always cut canvas in a straight line between the mesh and in a square or rectangular shape. This makes blocking easier. Bind the raw edges of the canvas with masking tape (see Figure 2–3a). Rub the handle of the scissors over the tape to make it stick better (see Figure 2–3b). Canvas ravels easily after the sizing is softened through handling. Tape *now;* once the raveling begins, it's too late. Even though Interlock Mono doesn't ravel readily, yarn and your clothes can snag on the canvas's raw edges.

If you don't work on a frame, carefully roll the canvas so you can easily reach your stitches (see Figure 2–4). *Never* crumple the canvas. Carefully pin the roll with large safety pins.

**Fig. 2-3a** *Bind the edges of the canvas with masking tape.*

**Fig. 2-3b** *Rub the handle of the scissors over the tape.*

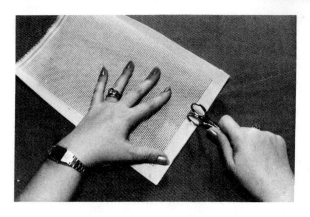

Needlepoint canvas is very rough. Pulling the yarn in and out of hole after hole wears it thin. Thin yarn produces skimpy stitches. So those stitches made at the beginning of a fresh strand of yarn will be plumper than those made at the end. *But* if you carefully watch the length of the strands you stitch with, this thinning can be controlled. Use a strand 18″ to 20″ long on 10, 12, or 14 canvas. You can use a longer strand for larger canvas and for Bargello (the stitches are long). On the other hand, though, you need a shorter strand on smaller canvas. Also remember that novelty yarns need to be quite short.

When Persian yarn comes in bulk, the strands are about 66″ or so long. Cut these strands into *thirds* for 10, 12, and 14 canvas (except Bargello). Cut them in *half* for larger canvas and Bargello. For those kinds of Persian yarn that comes in skeins, untwist the skein and cut the 66″circumference circle once. Then cut as described above.

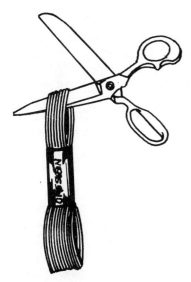

**Fig. 2-5** *Cutting a skein of yarn*

When tapestry yarn comes like the skein shown in Figure 2–5, merely cut the loops at one end and leave the label on. You can then pull one strand of yarn at a time by pulling from the looped end.

Some yarns are not packaged so that you can cut them as I've just described. Wrap the yarn around a book or box that measures 18″–20″ in circumference. Cut the yarn once. Then knot the yarn for storage.

## Finding the nap of the yarn

Yarn has *nap*. This means that it is smoother one way than the other. Look closely at the ends of a strand of yarn that has been cut for twenty-four hours or more before. You should be able to see that one end has relaxed or spread out more than the other. This fat end is called the Blooming End (see Figure 2–6). Put this end through the eye of the needle; then the nap of the yarn will be running correctly for the smoothest stitching. But before you thread the needle, you should strip the yarn.

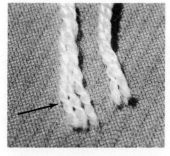

**Fig. 2-6** *The Blooming End*

## Stripping the yarn

**Fig. 2-7** *Stripping yarn*

Stripping the yarn makes Persian yarn plumper. Shipping crushes the yarn considerably. A plumper yarn covers the canvas better. Stripping is merely separating the three plies of Persian yarn and putting them back together again. (Tapestry yarn is not stripped.) Hold the Blooming End between the fingers of one hand and run two fingers between the three plies (see Figure 2–7).

Stripping gives you a double check on the nap. Once in a while it's hard to see which end is blooming. If you're holding the Blooming End, the strand will strip easily. If it does not, turn the strand of yarn upside down and do it again.

After you've stripped the yarn, run your hand down the strand two or three times. (Don't let go of the Blooming End yet.) This *stroking* of the yarn will get the extra fuzzies off. Stroke until they're gone.

## Thickening and thinning the yarn

**Fig. 2-8** *Stitches on the left show yarn so thin it does not cover canvas. Stitches on the right were worked with thickened yarn and cover the canvas properly.*

The thickness of the yarn must be adjusted according to the size of your canvas and the type of stitch you're using. Because the thickness of yarn varies with its type (tapestry or Persian), brand, and color, I can't tell you to always use a certain number of ply with a certain stitch and be sure that it will always cover the canvas.

Yarn must, therefore, be thickened or thinned to get proper canvas coverage. This is *much* easier with Persian yarn. To thicken, merely add one or two plies from another strand of yarn to a stripped 3-ply strand. Don't thicken too much. The stitch pattern can be obliterated, or the canvas can bulge. This is bad. To thin, just remove one or two plies. Play with your stitches, yarn, and canvas to get the proper combination for your project (see Figure 2–8).

Sometimes adding one ply makes the yarn too thick and subtracting one makes the yarn too thin, causing the canvas to show. This *grin-through* of canvas can be reduced by painting the canvas.

Another trick in covering the canvas is to add French knots (see page 149) or a Backstitch. If you're through stitching and you realize that you should have used one more ply, you can stitch right over what you've just done with one ply! Unfortunately this only works with simple stitches that don't cross each other.

When stitching Diagonal Stitches on Mono 14, only two

*SUPPLIES & BASIC PROCEDURES*

plies of Persian yarn are needed. So one ply is removed and saved. The other two are used to stitch. The odd ply is then placed with another odd one and also used for stitching. Sometimes the yarn covers the canvas, and sometimes it doesn't. This can be fixed.

Study a strand of Persian yarn. The three plies are *not* of equal weight. There is a fat, a medium, and a skinny ply. If you always lay aside the medium when you separate (or thin) the yarn, you will have yarns more equal in thickness than when you thinned haphazardly (see Figure 2–9). So one fat and one skinny together are about the same weight as two mediums. Now each 2-ply strand should cover almost as well as the one before.

HINT   If you're having trouble telling which strand is which, put a little tension on the strands. It sometimes helps, but if it doesn't, it won't make much difference which you choose.

Fig. 2-9a   *Fat, Medium, and Skinny plies in a strand of yarn.*

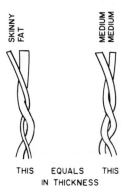

Fig. 2-9b   *One skinny and one fat = two mediums.*

## Using the yarn

Once you've threaded the needle, fold the yarn nearly in half (see Figure 2–10). Move the needle along the yarn as you stitch, so as not to wear a thin spot in the yarn. When using velour yarn, do just the opposite. Start with the needle about an inch from the end of the yarn. The canvas doesn't wear the velour yarn thin, but the needle does wear the yarn rather badly at the eye. Keep moving the needle in on the yarn (instead of out toward the end). As you will soon see, every bit of velour yarn past the eye must be thrown away. Be frugal.

As you stitch, try to keep the same twist on the yarn that you started with. As the yarn becomes untwisted or too tightly

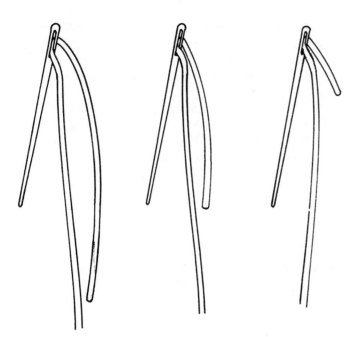

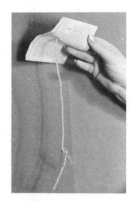

Fig. 2-11a *When the yarn becomes tightly twisted during stitching, turn the canvas upside down.*

Fig. 2-10 *Move the needle along the yarn as you stitch.*

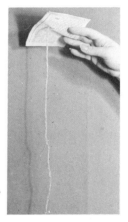

Fig. 2-11b *Let the needle dangle until the yarn untwists.*

twisted, hold the canvas upside down and let the needle dangle (see Figure 2–11). It will return automatically to its proper twist.

The stitches you choose cause the yarn to twist or untwist. As you become more experienced, you should be able to turn the needle enough as you stitch to correct the twist.

## Beginning and ending yarns

*Never* knot the yarn in needlepoint. To start the first yarn on a blank canvas, pull the yarn through to the right side of the canvas, leaving a good inch-long tail on the wrong side. As you make the first few stitches, catch the tail (see Figure 2–12). Work over the tail until it is covered.

Fig. 2-12 *Burying the tail*

There *is* one exception to using a knot in needlepoint—the *waste knot*. Use it when working on a frame or when working with a very slippery yarn (such as rayon) that won't hold a buried tail. First, knot the yarn (see Figure 2–13a–d). Next, put the needle *down* into the canvas from the right side, leaving the knot on the right side. Bring the needle up to the right side of the canvas about an inch from the knot. Place this re-entry point so that your first few stitches will catch this tail. When you come to the knot, merely cut it off from the right side of the canvas (see Figure 2–14).

Fig. 2-13a *To make a good, easy knot quickly, place the end of yarn over the eye of the needle.*

Fig. 2-13b *Wrap the yarn around the needle three times.*

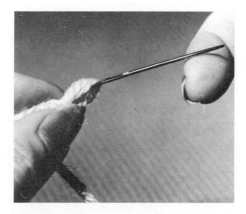

Fig. 2-13c *Pull the wrapped yarn over the eye of the needle and down the yarn.*

Fig. 2-13d *And presto! A knot!*

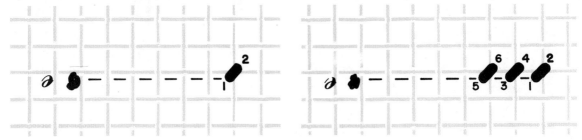

**Fig. 2-14a** *Using the waste knot*          **Fig. 2-14b**

To end a yarn, simply weave it over and under the back side of the stitches you've just worked. Clip the yarn closely (see Figure 2–15a).

You may begin subsequent yarns by weaving the tails under stitches you have already worked—on the wrong side, naturally. Try to bury tails within the same color. This makes it easier in case you have to rip (hope not!). Never bury a dark-colored yarn under light-colored stitches. It *will* show on the right side.

Long, loose stitches (such as Bargello) and stitches that have a lot of stress (such as Spider Webs and the Binding Stitch) *need* a firmer anchor for their yarn tails than do most other stitches. A Bargello tuck (or two sometimes) will give them the extra security they need (see Figure 2–15b). It's nothing but a back stitch taken after the tail has been woven in and before the needle goes through to the right side of the canvas.

Don't stop or start your yarn in a line or pattern. It *will* show on the right side. Also—do *not* carry your yarn from one area of stitching to another for more than 1″ to 1½″. And when you do carry it over for a few stitches, weave it into the backs of those stitches you're skipping.

**Fig. 2-15a** *Clip the ends of the yarn closely after burying the tails. This makes a neat back. Long ends are messy, get caught in other stitches, and make lumps on the right side of the canvas.*

**Fig. 2-15b** *A Bargello tuck*

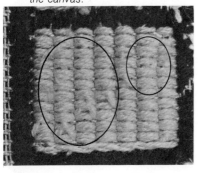

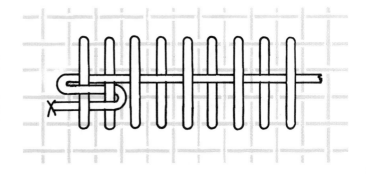

# Rolling the yarn

Sometimes one stitch on the same strand of yarn does not cover the canvas. This happens when the plies of the yarn are overly twisted or when they don't lie smoothly on the canvas. *Rolling* the yarn fixes this.

Use two hands—one on top of the canvas and the other underneath. Smooth the plies of yarn with either your fingers or another needle (see Figure 2–16a–e). This technique

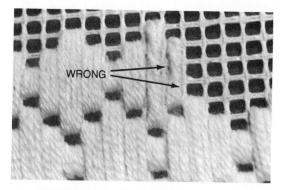

**Fig. 2-16a** *Wrong stitches need rolling*

**Fig. 2-16b** *Rolling yarn with the needle*

**Fig. 2-16 c&d** *Rolling yarn with your fingers.*

**Fig. 2-16e**

gives a much more professional-looking stitch. Rolling is very important when working with embroidery floss, rayon floss, and silk.

## Continuous motion versus stab method

*Continuous motion* is like sewing—the needle goes into and out of the canvas all in one smooth motion (see Figure 2–17). You can develop rhythm, speed, and even stitch tension with continuous motion when you work without a frame. However, if you work with a frame, the canvas should be so taut that you *cannot* stitch in a continuous motion. If you do use this method with a frame, you might as well put the frame away. Unless the canvas is taut, you cannot get the full benefits of a frame.

The *stab method* is used with a frame and on plastic canvas. Your dominant hand is constantly below the canvas and the other hand is on top of the canvas. Both hands work together when the frame is independently supported. But when you're using a frame you have to hold or when you're working on plastic canvas, use the method shown in Figure 2–18.

**Fig. 2-17** *Continuous motion*

**Fig. 2-18 a&b** *Stab method*

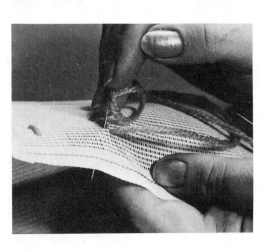
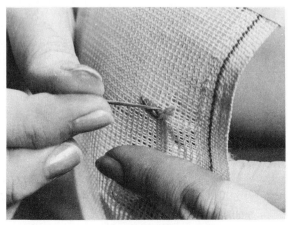

## Direction of work

Whenever you can, bring the needle *up* into an empty hole and *down* into a full hole. This helps to cut down on splitting the yarn. Keep in mind that you don't always have a choice. Don't knock yourself out trying to achieve the impossible.

## Tension

The tension of your stitches should be even. Each stitch should hug the canvas, not choke it. See examples of correct tension and too tight and too loose tension in Figure 2–19a–c. Don't mistake a ripple of the canvas (when the stitch tension is too tight) for the distortion that some stitches cause. In the case of distortion, the canvas lies fairly flat on the table. Notice that long stitches need to be pulled more tightly than shorter one (see "Mosaic and Scotch Stitches" on pages 120 and 125).

Never use stitches that distort (See charts in Part III) on projects that do not have a rigid framework to hold the canvas permanently in place. The Diagonal Stitches and the Box Stitches are the worst offenders in canvas distortion.

**Fig. 2-19a** *Correct tension*

**Fig. 2-19b** *Too-tight tension*

**Fig. 2-19c** *Too-loose tension*

## Direction of stitches

In stitching a needlepoint piece, work the design first. Then stitch the background. The stitch you choose will determine where you start the background. Don't skip around with the background stitch, for the pattern probably won't meet.

## Compensating stitches

Whenever you use a decorative stitch, there's always some space between the last whole motif of your stitch and the edge of the remaining area to be covered. The space must be filled with as much of the motif as you can muster. The stitches that fill those areas are called *compensating stitches*.

In beginning to stitch a decorative stitch, establish your pattern across the widest part of your design area. Work as many whole motifs as you can. Then go back and do the compensating stitches (see Figure 2–20).

Try to work as much of the motif as you can. Then stop on your line. To help you see the compensating stitches that you need, lay a piece of paper over the stitch drawing where you need it. Hold your needlepoint to the light to check for missed stitches.

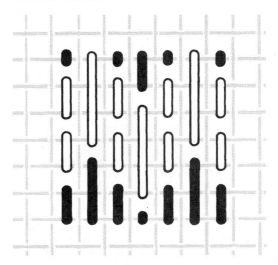

**Fig. 2-20**  *The black stitches are the compensating stitches for Hungarian stitch (page 98).*

## Mixing diagonal and vertical stitches

Diagonal stitches and vertical stitches do not mix well together without a little trick. Work the diagonal stitches first. Then stitch a row of tent stitches around the diagonal stitches in the same color as the vertical stitches. Then work the vertical stitches, sharing the hole (see Figure 2–21).

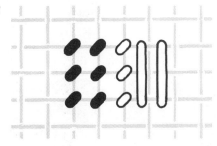

**Fig. 2-21** *Mixing diagonal and vertical stitches*

## Ripping and mending

Blessed is a cheerful ripper! Figure 2–22 shows how to rip correctly.

*NEVER* reuse yarn that you have carefully ripped. It's much to fuzzy by now to use again.

Now that the wrong stitches are out, you'll have to rip a few good ones in order to have enough yarn to bury the tails. A crochet hook makes burying these short tails easy.

If you have cut the canvas, all you have to do is cut a patch and put it under the cut, matching the mesh exactly (see Figure 2–23a). Then stitch through both thicknesses of canvas as if they were one (see Figure 2–23b). Be sure the patch is on the wrong side of the canvas.

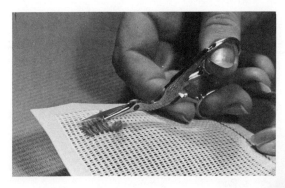

**Fig. 2-22a** *To rip, cut the* wrong *stitches on the* right *side of the canvas. (Be careful not to cut the canvas.)*

**Fig. 2-22b** *With tweezers, pull out the incorrect stitches from the wrong side of the canvas.*

**Fig. 2-23a** *To mend cut canvas, cut a patch of the same kind of canvas slightly bigger than the hole.*

**Fig. 2-23b** *Stitch through both thicknesses on the canvas as if they were one piece. (The wrong side of the mended area is shown in the photo.)*

## Cleaning needlepoint

Needlepoint can be cleaned. Washing in cold water with mild soap is recommended. This does remove some sizing, and the canvas loses its stiffness and, thus, some strength. So don't be over-zealous in washing.

Rinse well. Roll in terry cloth towels. Block immediately (see page 157).

Do not use any commercial cleaners or protectors. Colors have run, and wool and canvas may rot prematurely.

## Instructions for left-handers

Left-handed people *can* do needlepoint. Most of my left-handed students had learned to adapt to a right-handed world before they got to me.

Some useful hints: Reverse "right" and "left" and "up" and "down". Hold the canvas any way you have to in order to get the right results (see Figure 2–24).

**Fig. 2-24 a-b** *Left-handers, take the diagram shown in (a) and simply turn it upside down as shown in (b).*

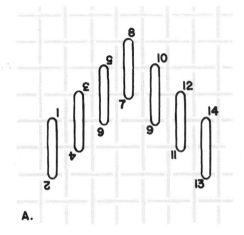

**A.**

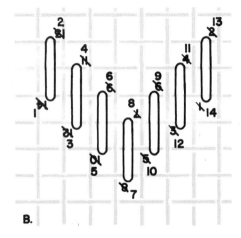

**B.**

Most of the patterns in this book will need to be enlarged before you can use them. A *lithographer* can do it for you (check the Yellow Pages). Or you can do it yourself if you have more time than money. Use the *grid method.* Draw ¼″ squares on your design (or on a traced copy). Draw 1″ squares on another piece of paper. Copy the lines inside each square. You have just increased the drawing four times—all by yourself! By changing the size of the squares, you can vary the size of the final design (see Figure 2–25).

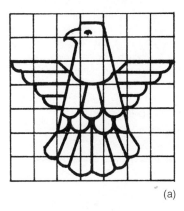

(a)

**Fig. 2-25 a-c** *Grid method of enlarging and reducing designs.*

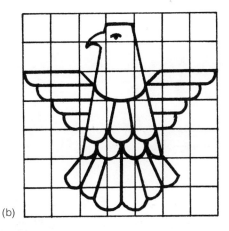

(b)

(c)

Once your design is the right size, you can put it onto canvas very easily (see Figure 2–26, a–j).

Use a *waterproof grey* marker to trace the outline of the design onto the canvas. Fill in with appropriate colors. You might like to use acrylic paint instead of markers. Hints for working with paint follow.

1. Thin your paint with water to the consistency of liquid dishwashing detergent. Use an eye dropper to keep from adding too much water. It's better that the paint be too thick rather than too thin. Ideally, the paint should not come through on to the wrong side of the canvas, nor should it clog the holes.
2. Use a broad, stiff brush for large areas and a fine, stiff one for small areas. Keep the brush pretty dry. You don't want to dissolve the sizing on the canvas.
3. White (or tan) paint makes a good eraser. Cover your error with paint that is the same color as your canvas. Let it dry. Then paint right over it.
4. Use separate cans of water for each color. It saves lots of trips to the sink. Soup cans work well.
5. Mix the paint in a throw-away container, such as a styrofoam egg carton.
6. Clean-up with acrylic paint is easy—use soap and water.
7. Finally, spray the canvas with a fixative to set the paint.

Now that you know the basics, go on to the fun—creating your own projects, using my ideas—or yours!

**Fig. 2-26a** *Supplies needed to ready a canvas for stitching.*

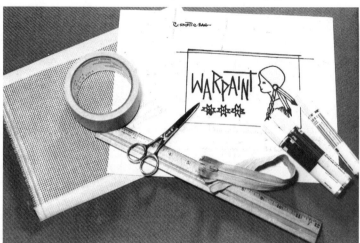

*SUPPLIES & BASIC PROCEDURES*

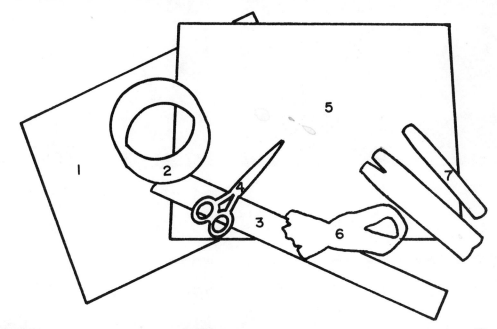

Fig. 2-26b *(1) canvas, (2) masking tape, (3) ruler, (4) scissors, (5) drawing of design, (6) zipper (used in this case to get correct size for a make-up bag), and (7) waterproof markers—if used instead of acrylic paints.*

Fig. 2-26c *Bind the edges of the canvas with masking tape.*

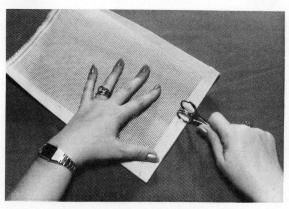

Fig. 2-26d *Rub the handle of a pair of scissors over the tape to make it stick better.*

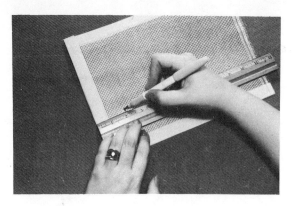

**Fig. 2-26e** *Mark two of the margins.*

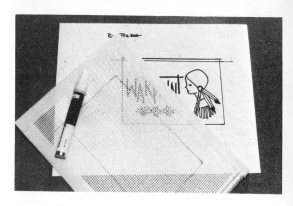

**Fig. 2-26f** *Trace your drawing with a black marker.*

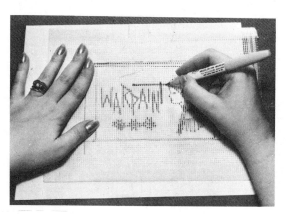

**Fig. 2-26g** *Lay the canvas over the design, and trace it onto the canvas with a waterproof grey marker.*

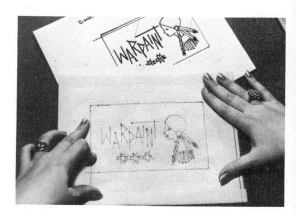

**Fig. 2-26h** *Your canvas should look like this.*

**Fig. 2-26i** *Paint the background. Let it dry.*

**Fig. 2-26j** *The canvas is now ready to stitch.*

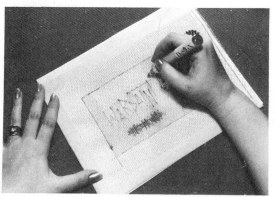

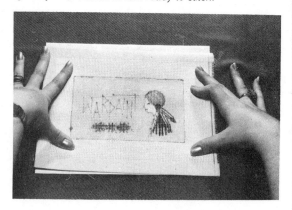

*SUPPLIES & BASIC PROCEDURES*

PART TWO

# MAKING SOMETHING FROM NOTHING

Making something out of nothing can be a satisfying experience or a disaster. The trick in success is to do it in style and with a flair. I've tried to select projects that won't look as though you've started with nothing.

It's again time for my lectures on finishing. I firmly believe that expert finishing spells the difference between homemade and hand-made. Mediocre stitching will be overlooked if the finishing is professional, yet flawless stitching will be overpowered by poor finishing.

To help scrap projects look their best, I must encourage you to choose prefinished articles, such as a tote bag or a card case. Although they make finishing easier, a little time and effort will enable you to make other nicely finished projects. Don't overlook Part IV of this book—It's on finishing.

Chapter three

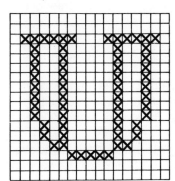 SING SCRAPS
OF YARN
& CANVAS

This chapter is made up of projects that use both yarn and canvas scraps. You need not have scraps on hand, but if you do, here are a few good ways to use them.

## Address file box

STITCHES:  Continental

CANVAS:  Mono 18, 4½″ × 6″ (½″ margins included)

YARN:  Persian

NEEDLE:  Size 22

SIZE OF FINISHED PROJECT:  3½″ × 5″

This box top is stiched on a special canvas, called Congress Cloth, that comes in many colors. The background does not necessarily have to be stitched. A smaller canvas, say 22 mesh per inch, will enable you to achieve a more detailed design. But I used this size because this was what I had in *my* scrap bag!

The design I chose is an addressed letter. You may make your own by X-ing in squares on a sheet of graph paper. Each square equals one Continental Stitch. This is called a graphed or charted design.

Before stitching, locate the center of the canvas by folding it in half and then in half again. Find the center of the graph chart. Begin stitching there. Each X represents one Continental Stitch (see Figure 3–1c). Other symbols are used to indicate different colors. During stitching, treat each symbol as if it were an X.

Be careful not to carry the yarn from one area to another when you are not planning to stitch the background. Begin and end each stitch neatly (see "Basic Procedures," page 26).

Block as described on page 157. Lace the canvas over cardboard (see page 168) and glue onto the top of a wooden file box. Finish the edge with a twisted cord (see page 171). Tuck in the ends of the cord neatly.

**Fig. 3-1a** *File Box*

*MAKING SOMETHING FROM NOTHING*

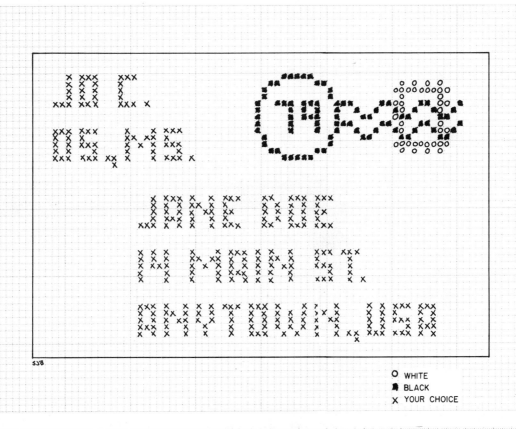

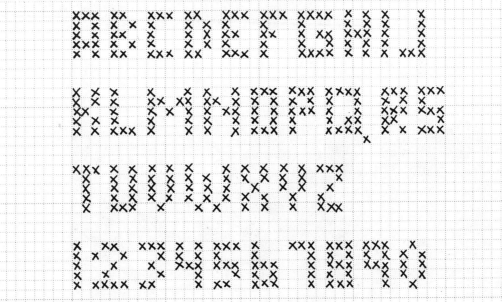

**Fig. 3-1b** *Graph chart File Box*

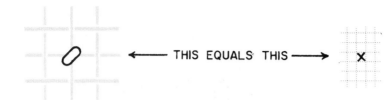

**Fig. 3-1c** *Continental stitch on canvas and on graph paper.*

THIS EQUALS THIS

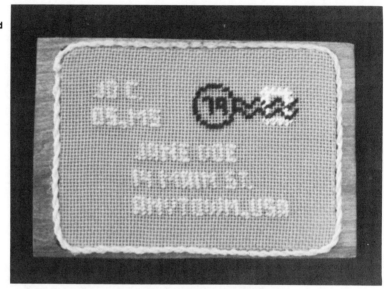

**Fig. 3-1d**

**Fig. 3-1e** *Close-up*

*MAKING SOMETHING FROM NOTHING*

# Round box

STITCHES: 1. Straight—pattern of your choice
2. Binding


CANVAS: Plastic; two 3″ circles; one long strip 10¼″ × 2″, satin lining.

YARN: Persian

NEEDLE: Size 18

SIZE OF FINISHED PROJECT: 3¼″ × 2″

Simple Straight Stitches with thickened yarn cover the plastic canvas for this box. Follow Figure 3–2b or make up your own design. No blocking is necessary.

Attach beads to single-ply yarn and sew them to the inside of the top, near the edge. Line each piece separately with a padded lining (see page 172). Join the ends of the long piece together with the Binding Stitch. Sew the bottom of the box to the sides with the Binding Stitch. Stitch the Binding Stitch around the top edges of the sides. Leave about ¾″ blank. This will be the hinge. End the yarn. Then stitch the Binding Stitch around the edges of the lid. Begin this yarn at

**Fig. 3-2a**  *Round box*

**Fig. 3-2b**  *Plastic circle, alternate design*

point A in Figure 3–2c and stitch to point B. To this point you have stitched through only one thickness of plastic canvas. Now lay the lid on the box, matching the blank areas. Continuing with the same yarn, work the Binding Stitch through both pieces of canvas. Secure the end well. This is the hinge.

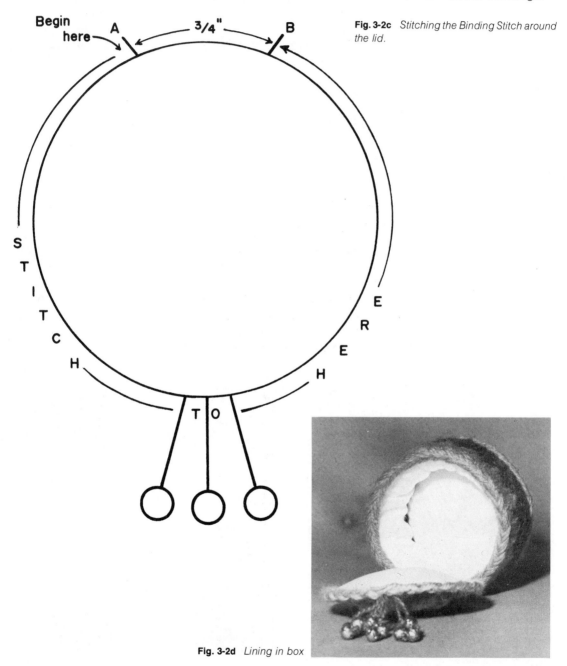

**Fig. 3-2c** *Stitching the Binding Stitch around the lid.*

**Fig. 3-2d** *Lining in box*

MAKING SOMETHING FROM NOTHING

# Rainbow case

STITCHES:  1. Diagonal Cashmere
               2. Binding

CANVAS:  Plastic 7

YARN:  Persian

NEEDLE:  Size 18

SIZE OF FINISHED PROJECT:

This case can hold any number of things, from cigarettes to calculators to remote controls.

    The theory is the same; only the measuring is different. Allow one mesh all the way around your item for the Binding Stitch and another mesh for ease (see Figure 3–3c). Stitch with the Diagonal Cashmere in a rainbow pattern or in any stitch or colors you like.

    Line each piece separately. Sew the seams together and finish the edges that are not seams with the Binding Stitch.

**Fig. 3-3a**  *Rainbow case*

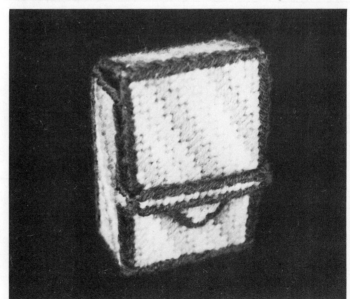

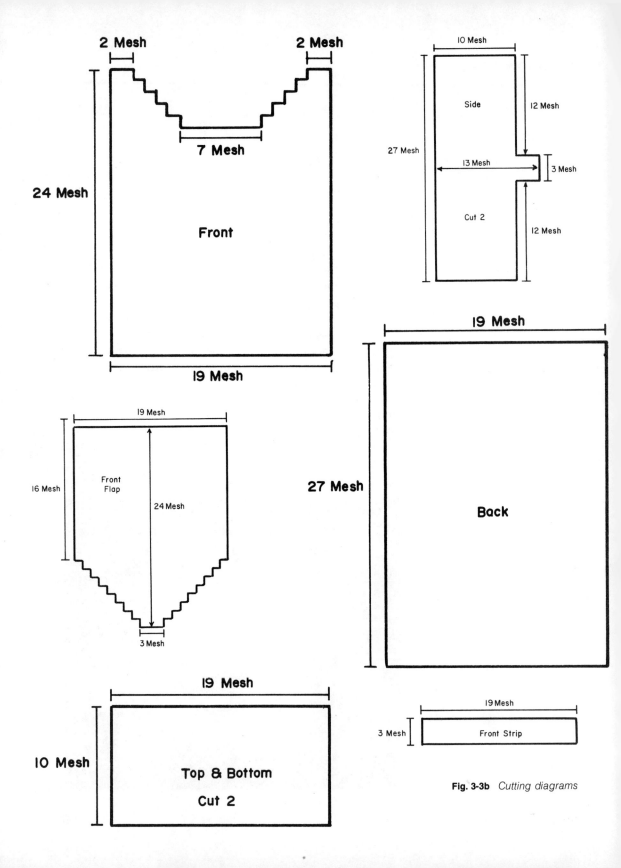

**2 Mesh**     **2 Mesh**

7 Mesh

24 Mesh

Front

19 Mesh

10 Mesh

Side

12 Mesh

27 Mesh

13 Mesh

3 Mesh

Cut 2

12 Mesh

19 Mesh

Front
Flap

16 Mesh

24 Mesh

3 Mesh

27 Mesh

19 Mesh

Back

19 Mesh

Top & Bottom

10 Mesh

Cut 2

19 Mesh

3 Mesh

Front Strip

**Fig. 3-3b** *Cutting diagrams*

**Fig. 3-3c** *How to measure for another item*

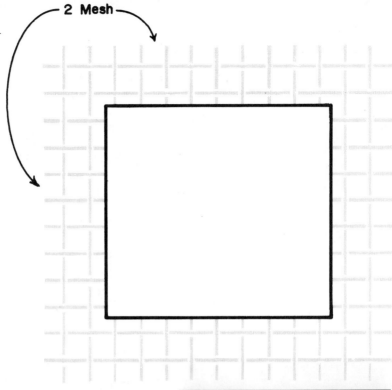
**2 Mesh**

**Fig. 3-3d** *Close-up*

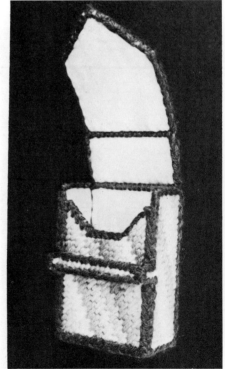

**Fig. 3-3e** *Lining the case*

*Using Scraps of Yarn and Canvas*

# Dove

STITCHES:  1. Split Stitch
                2. Basketweave
                3. Hungarian
                4. Parisian

CANVAS:   Interlock Mono, 14, 7" x 7" (3" margins included)

YARN:   Persian or tapestry; embroidery floss (dove)

NEEDLE:   Size 20

SIZE OF FINISHED PROJECT:   4" × 4"

Work the background first and then stitch the dove. Ignore the mesh and plant the stitch so that it follows the shape of the dove.

    Block (see page 157). Stretch over a piece of plywood as described in the chapter on Framing (see page 162). Have your frame surround the plywood with molding. The framed neelepoint can then be glued onto a framed mirror.

**Fig. 3-4a** *Dove*

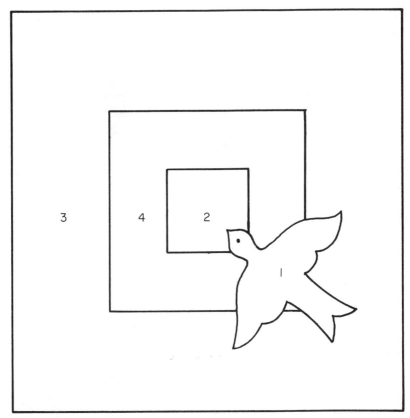

**Fig. 3-4b**

3     4     2

1

**Fig. 3-4c** *Close-up*

# Mouse and cheese

STITCHES:   1. Reversed Mosaic
                2. Straight Gobelin
                3. Continental (outlines)
                4. Reversed Scotch
                5. Brick
                6. Basketweave
                7. French Knots

CANVAS:   Mono 10, 9″ × 14¼″, Nylon 20, small scraps (3″ margins included)

YARN:   Persian—thicken for Brick Stitch, Thin for nylon canvas

NEEDLE:   Sizes 20 and 22

SIZE OF FINISHED PROJECT:   3″ × 8¼″

This piece has a raised mouse, swiss cheese and a small hunk of cheese. These items are stitched on separate pieces of canvas (Nylon 20) that are then appliqued onto the background canvas. Just before closing the stitching off, the areas are stuffed.

Stitch the design on both pieces of canvas separately. Allow a ½″ margin around the mouse and cheese pieces, but do not trim the canvas yet. Work the background and design on the large canvas to within ⅝″ of the pieces to be appliqued.

Block all pieces (see page 157). Now trim the nylon canvas pieces to within ½″ of the stitching. Melt the edges of the nylon canvas with a match. The edges will not ravel now.

Baste the mouse and cheese pieces securely onto the background canvas. They're a little bigger and will have to be eased in. Just before closing off the hole, stuff the mouse with polyester fiber. Be careful not to overstuff. The canvas should lie flat on a table.

Stitch the background through both thicknesses of canvas as if they were one. Follow the mesh of the bigger canvas to maintain the stitch size. If you're having trouble seeing the larger canvas's mesh, hold it up to the light to see where to put the needle. Because the nylon is so thin, no

**Fig. 3-5a** *Mouse and Cheese*

ridge will show. If bits of nylon canvas peek through your stitches, just snip them off.

Mount the finished design on a piece of plywood (see page 168).

**Fig. 3-5b**

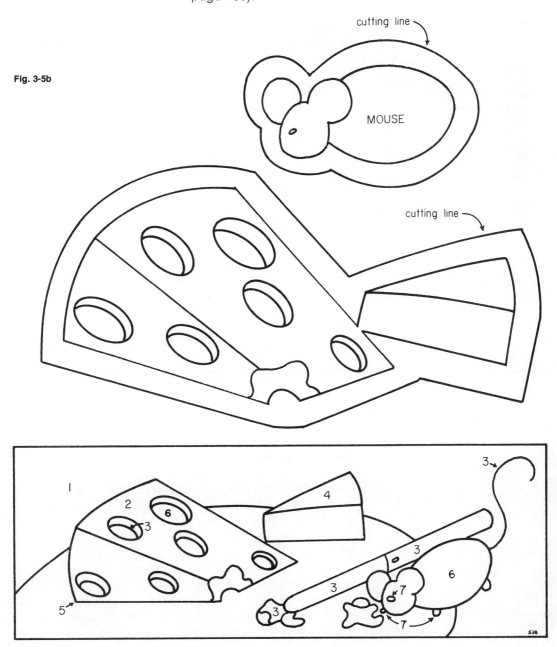

**Fig. 3-5c** *Close-up*

# Basket of strawberries

STITCHES: 1. Mosaic
2. Running
3. Horizonal Old Florentine
4. Turkey Work
5. Straight

CANVAS: Plastic 10 (basket): bottom 4″ × 4″, four sides, each 3″ × 4″ Interlock Mono 10 (strawberries and blossoms)

YARN: Tapestry or Persian, pearl cotton for Running Stitch

NEEDLE: Size 20

SIZE OF FINISHED PROJECT: 4″ × 4″ × 3″

The basket pictured here has slanting sides. Mickey found the corners hard to stitch and still cover the canvas. If you wish to slant the sides, it will look more like a basket; however, Mickey and I recommend that beginners stick with the measurements listed above. Stitch and line each piece separately (see page 172).

Each of the strawberries can be made from miscellaneous pieces of scrap canvas. Not all of the strawberries need to be the same size or even the same exact shape. The bigger the canvas you have for the strawberries, the easier blocking will be.

Stitch and block as many strawberries as you wish. Trim to within ¼". Using a whip stitch, sew the side seam on each strawberry. Leave the top open for now. Stuff with sachet or polyester fiber. Put a Running Stitch in and out around the tops of the strawberries. Pull both ends tightly and tie securely. Cut a calyx out of green felt. Knot a green yarn. Run it through the center of the calyx. Cut a blossom out of blank white interlock Mono canvas. Attach it to the green yarn with yellow yarn in a Turkey Work pattern.

Use individual strawberries as sachets, gifts, package decorations, or Christmas tree ornaments!

**Fig. 3-6a** *Basket of Strawberries*

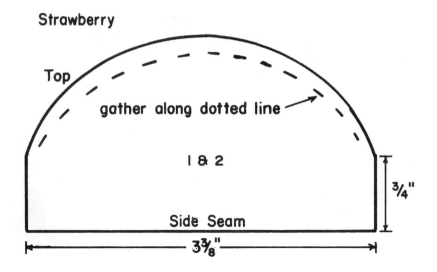

**Strawberry**

Top

gather along dotted line

I & 2

Side Seam

¾"

3⅜"

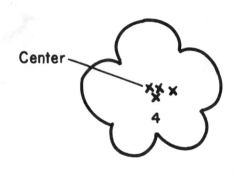

Center

X X X
X

4

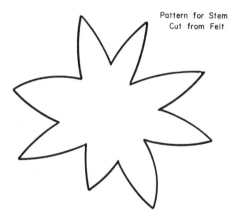

Pattern for Stem
Cut from Felt

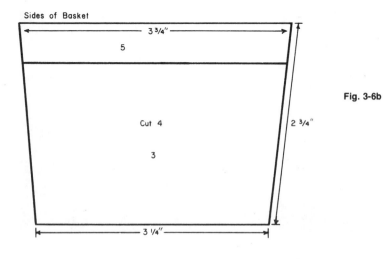

Sides of Basket

3 ¾"

5

Cut 4

3

2 ¾"

3 ¼"

**Fig. 3-6b**

## Bottom of Basket

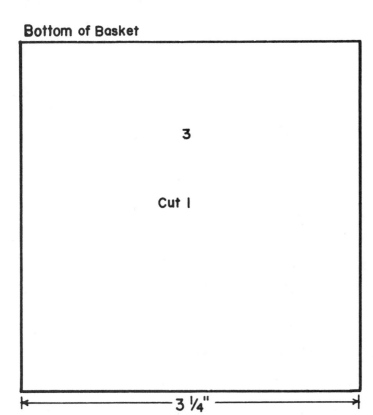

3

Cut I

⟵——————— 3 ¼" ———————⟶

**Fig. 3-6b** *(cont.)*

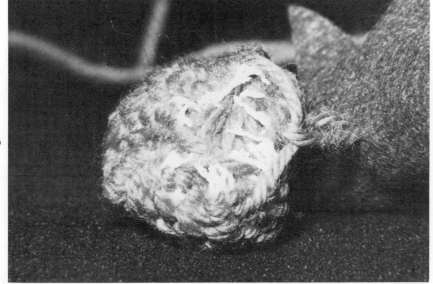

**Fig. 3-6c** *Close-up*

Chapter four

# ESIGNING WITH SCRAPS OF YARN

This chapter is comprised of projects that employ scrap yarn for the design, but not for the background. No canvas scraps were used.

## Briefcase

STITCHES:
1. Continental
2. Basketweave
3. Three-Stitch Cross
4. Smyrna
5. Greek Stitch
6. Fern

CANVAS: Interlock Mono 12, 4″ x 7″ (in prefinished Brief-case)

YARN: Persian

NEEDLE: Size 20

SIZE OF FINISHED PROJECT: 4″ × 7″

This charted design is really easier than it looks. The border is merely rows of decorative stitches. The alphabet given here is merely a suggestion. Try one of your own, if you like. Be sure to center the monogram in the area given in a pre-finished piece.

This project cannot be blocked without ruining the suede briefcase. This is true of almost all prefinished items, so you need to choose stitches carefully in order to avoid distortion.

Many prefinished pieces include a lining to cover the back of your stitching. If not, it would be nice for you to tack a lining in place.

**Fig. 4-1a** *Briefcase*

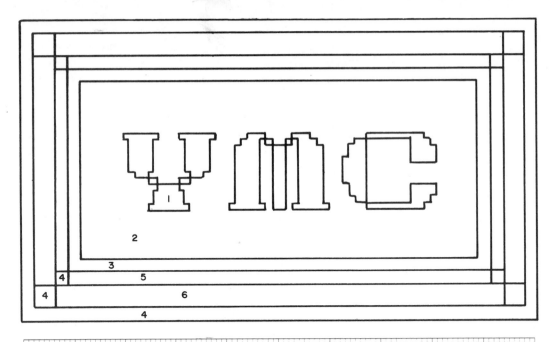

**Fig. 4-1b** *Alphabet*

**Fig. 4-1c** *Close-up*

# Sampler pillow

STITCHES:

1. Milanese
2. Oriental
3. Spaced Cross Tramé
4. Oblong Cross
5. Slanted Gobelin
6. Moorish
7. Diagonal Hungarian Ground
8. Jacquard
9. Scotch
10. Mosaic
11. Diagonal Cashmere
12. Parisian
13. Pavillion
14. Woven Scotch
15. Rice Giant
16. Double Cross
17. Diagonal Scotch
18. Hitched Cross
19. Cross (divider and monogram)
20. Byzantine
21. Basketweave

**Fig. 4-2a** *Sampler Pillow*

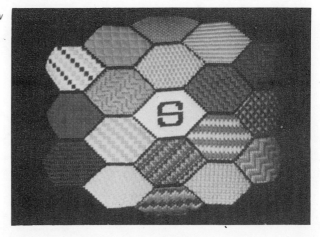

CANVAS: Interlock Mono 10, 18″ × 18″

YARN: Persian and tapestry

NEEDLE: 20

SIZE OF FINISHED PROJECT: 14″ × 14″

First stitch the black outline and then the monogram. Fill in with the suggested stitches or some of your choice.

Block (see page 157) and assemble into a pillow (see page 169).

**Fig. 4-2b** *Pillow*

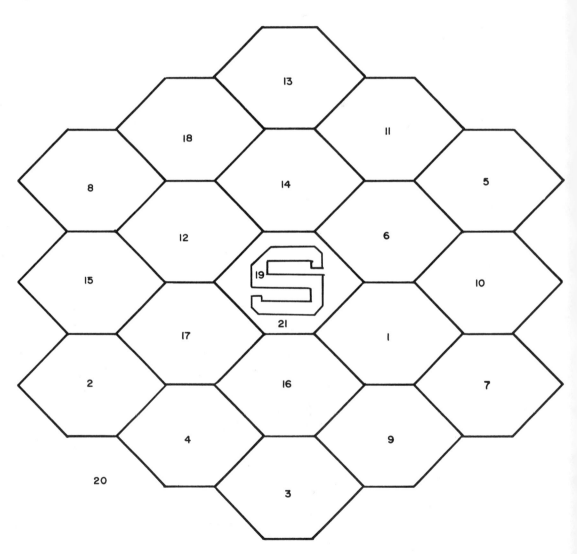

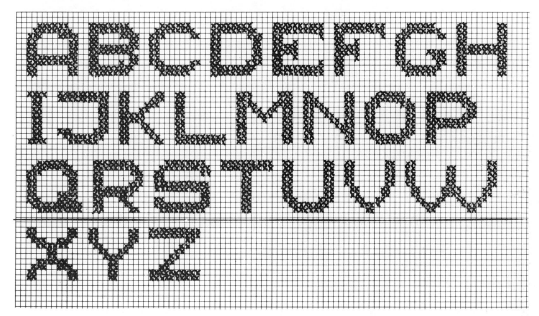

**Fig. 4-2c** *Alphabet*

## Computer tote bag

STITCHES:
1. Brick (overall background)
2. Running Stitch (lettering at bottom)
3. Upright Cross (computer and mouth)
4. Couching (computer)
5. Web (screen)
6. Continental (Happy Face, problem, letters, and numbers)
7. Smyrna (eyes)
8. Giant Brick (over 3) (graph)
9. Long Upright Cross (diskette and oblong hole)
10. Ringed Daisy (over 1 mesh) (round hole)
11. Lazy Kalem (background of each shape)

CANVAS: Interlocking Mono 12, 2¾″ × 13¾″ in prefinished tote bag

YARN: Persian

NEEDLE: Size 20

SIZE OF FINISHED PRODUCT: 2¾″ × 13¾

When stitching each design portion, work the background of each shape, then the design. It makes those portions more prominent.

Watch your tension, as you cannot block this piece. Line the back of your work.

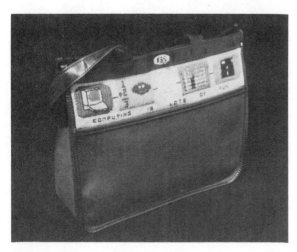

**Fig. 4-3a** *Computer Tote Bag*

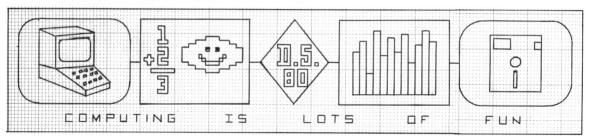

**Fig. 4-3b**

**Fig. 4-3c**
*Close-up*

Fig. 4-3d

## Crayon box

STITCHES: 1. Continental (outlines)
2. Basketweave
3. Upright Cross
4. Brick
5. Couching (smoke, fish)
6. Binding (on edges)
7. Straight (fish features)

CANVAS: Interlock Mono 14, 4½" × 8½" (½" margins allowed)

YARN: Persian

NEEDLE: Size 20

SIZE OF FINISHED PROJECT: 3½" × 8½"

The Two-step Edge-finishing Method allows us to finish a raw edge of canvas as we stitch. You must plan ahead, however. This also prepares the canvas for the Binding Stitch. Heretofore, we have put the Binding Stitch on plastic canvas, and we haven't needed to prepare the canvas.

You need six mesh all the way around the design when you are stitching on Mono canvas. Figure 4–4c shows you where those 6 mesh are.

Insert your needle under the 5th and 6th mesh. Fold the canvas so that these two mesh are on the *edge*. This will automatically make a four-mesh hem (see Figure 4–4e). You might want to baste this hem in place. If so, do it now. Be sure the mesh line up. Stitch through both thicknesses of the canvas as if they were one. Only the two-mesh edge for the Binding Stitch should show (see Figure 4–4f). Refer to the Binding Stitch on page 136).

Block with T-pins (see page 161). Glue the finished design to the box.

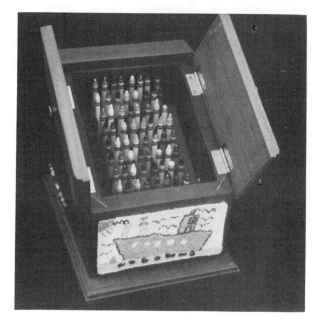

**Fig. 4-4a** *Crayon Box*

**Fig. 4-4b**

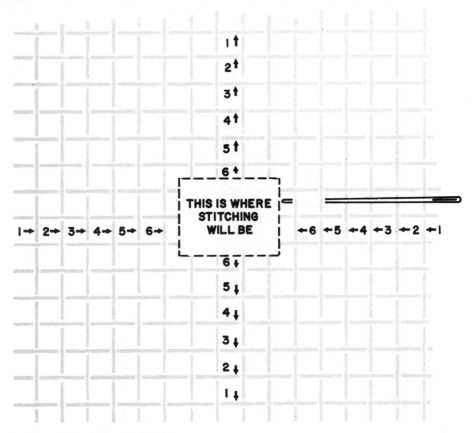

**Fig. 4-4c** *Finding mesh on Mono canvas edge for two-step finishing.*

**Fig. 4-4d** *How to cut canvas*

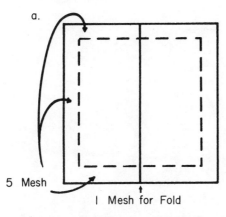

OR

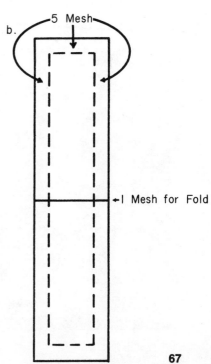

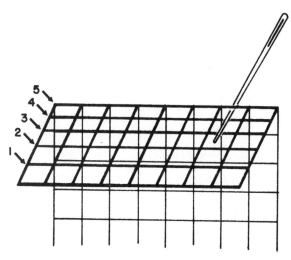

**Fig. 4-4e** *Folding canvas for Binding Stitch.*

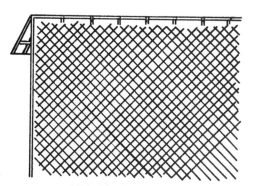

**Fig. 4-4f** *Stitch right up to the edge.*

**Fig. 4-4g**
*Close-up*

MAKING SOMETHING FROM NOTHING

**Fig. 4-4h**

**Fig. 4-4i** *Child's drawing*

*Designing with Scraps of Yarn*

Chapter five

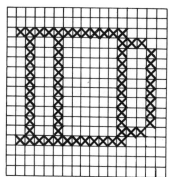 # ESIGNS &
# BACKGROUNDS
# WITH SCRAPS

The projects in this chapter are designed to use scrap yarn for both the design and the background. Projects using canvas scraps are not included.

## TV guide cover

---

STITCHES:  1. Reversed Cashmere
2. Continental
3. Binding Stitch

CANVAS:  Mono Interlock 10, 8¾″ × 12″ (½″ margins allowed)

YARN:  Tapestry

NEEDLE: Size 20

SIZE OF FINISHED PROJECT: 7¾" × 11"

Use the Two-Step Edge-finishing Method to finish the edges on this project. Don't forget you have to plan ahead (see page 65).

Next, position the lettering and stitch it. Leave two mesh blank for a spine. You'll put the Binding Stitch here later.

Stitch the background in diagonal rows with any color yarn you have. Stitch one strand at a time until the strand is gone. Then pick another color.

Block with T-pins (see page 161). Finish the edges and the spine with the Binding Stitch. Cut two pieces of light-weight cardboard slightly smaller than half of the needle-point. Line with one piece of fabric. Before closing one end, slip in one piece of cardboard. Using a Running Stitch, sew the lining down to the needlepoint along the spine. Slip in the other piece of cardboard and sew up the end (see Figure 5–1c). Sew a piece of elastic at points A and B.

Your *TV Guide* cover is now ready to slip onto the latest issue.

**Fig. 5-1a** *TV Guide Cover*

**Fig. 5-1b** *TV graph chart*

**Fig. 5-1c** *Lining and cardboard*

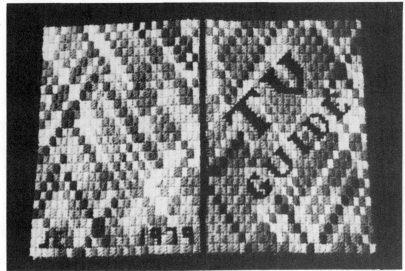

**Fig. 5-1d** *Front and back*

**Fig. 5-1e** *Close-up*

# Vase of flowers

STITCHES: 1. Ridged Spider Web
2. Needleweaving

CANVAS: None

YARN: Any kind—variety adds interest

NEEDLE:   Size 18

SIZE OF FINISHED PROJECT:   6″ × 3″

To make the flowers, cut a disk of cardboard 3¼″ × 3½″ in diameter. Make eight equally spaced notches around the edge. Cut about 3½ yards of yarn for each flower. Starting in the middle of the disk, hold one end of yarn and wrap it around and around the disk until each notch is filled. The yarn, thus, forms spokes. Using one end of the 3½-yard piece of yarn, tie a knot at the center of the spokes. Clip the shortest end to ½″. Thread the needle with the other end of the yarn and begin the Ridged Spider Web Stitch. Use all the yarn on the needle. Finish by running the threaded needle under the stitches on a ridge, toward the center. Leave this tail hanging. Turn the disk over. Cut all of the yarn spokes where they cross in the center. Fold these spokes down so that they meet the hanging center tail. You will now have a smooth rounded ball of yarn.

Make a stem of #20 florist wire. Bend one end down to form a hook. Insert this end of the wire into the flower. Hook a stitch in the center. Pull the tail downward with one hand and with the other push the eight spokes upward so that the flowers poof out. Wrap all nine pieces of yarn and the wire very tightly with green floral tape. Add a leaf or two as you wrap.

Use pipe cleaners as a form for leaves. Buy green pipe cleaners from a hobby shop or dye white ones with a green marker or with green dye. Shape them basically as shown in Figure 5–2c. Leave one end longer than the other to reduce bulk. Work needleweaving over this leaf-shaped form. Work as tightly or as loosely as you wish. Bury the tail between the stitches.

**Fig. 5-2a** *Vase of Flowers*

Many containers can be used, but the one shown in Figure 5–2 is a small relish jar. Fill the grooves at the top by wrapping the area with soft cotton twine. Then, starting at the bottom, wrap the jar tightly with jute twine. Glue the twine to the jar as you go with white glue. Push the rows together as your wrap. Glue a piece of felt to the bottom of the jar.

Pack the jar with vermiculite or a block of styrofoam. Arrange the flowers, distributing the colors evenly. Pour glue inside the jar to stabilize the flowers.

**Fig. 5-2b** *Disk for flower*

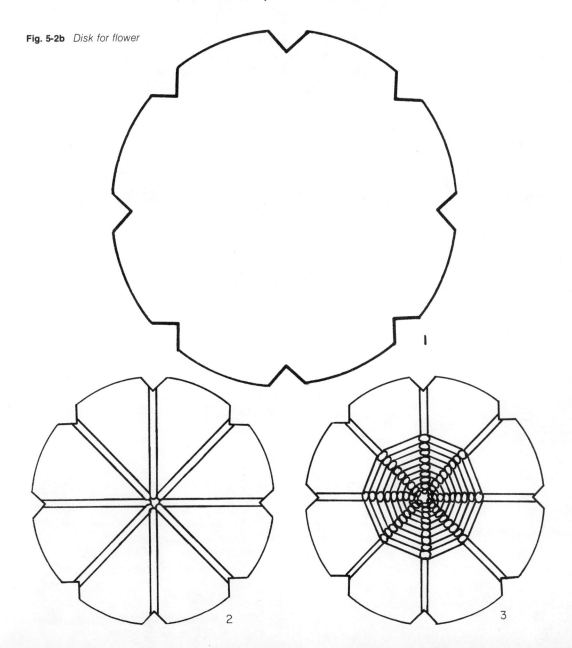

2

3

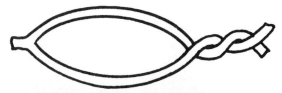

**Fig. 5-2c** *Making a leaf*

**Fig. 4-2d** *Close-up*

# Flowered eyeglass case

STITCHES:  1. Basketweave
            2. Binding Stitch
            3. Continental (outline)

CANVAS:  Interlock Mono 12, 3½″ × 6½″, or what you need for your glasses (½″ margin allowed)

YARN:  Persian

NEEDLE:  Size 20

SIZE OF FINISHED PROJECT: 3½″ × 6½″

Prepare your canvas for the Two-step Edge finish. Transfer your design onto the canvas.

This design is versatile in that it can be cut, enlarged, or reduced as you wish. Use it for an eyeglass case, a pillow, or even a vest.

The color scheme is easily changed according to what you have in your scrap bag.

A. Monochromatic—five (or more) shades of one family plus white background.
   1. Outline in the darkest shade.
   2. Fill in flowers at random with the other four shades.
   3. Work the background.
B. Pastel Color Scheme—dark brown background.
   1. Work background and outlines first in the darkest color.
   2. Fill in with pastel scraps.
C. Multi-color—medium color scheme.
   1. Outline the flower in one color.
   2. Work the flower centers in another color.
   3. Work the petals in a third color.
   4. Repeat Steps 1 to 3 for each flower, varying the color schemes as your stock pile permits.
   5. Work the background in a blending or contrasting color.
D. Rainbow—bright color scheme
   1. Work the outlines in black.
   2. Stitch the flower centers in gold.
   3. Fill in the rest with bright colors. Stitch with the Basketweave Stitch and change colors as you run out of one or as you want to change.
   4. Bind the edges in black.

Block with T-pins (see page 161). Line (see page 172). Sew the seams and finish the top edges with the Binding Stitch.

**Fig. 5-3a** *Flowered Eye Glass Cases*

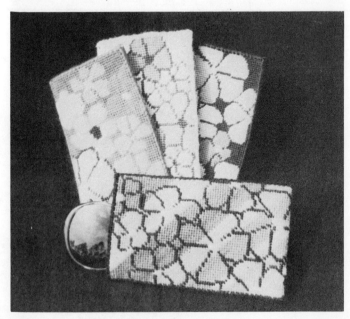

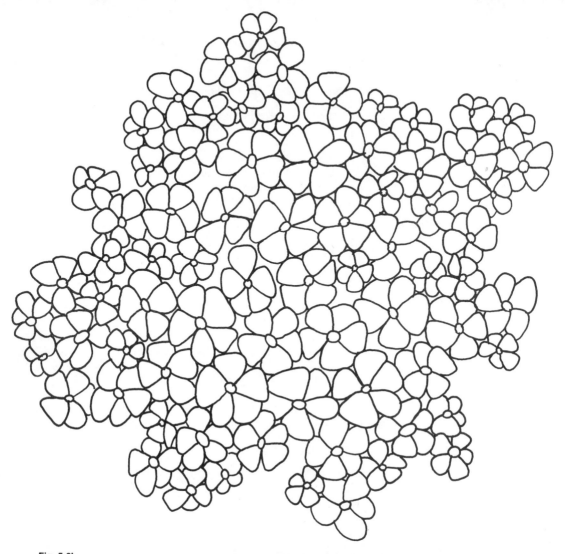

**Fig. 5-3b**

**Fig. 5-3c**  *Close-up*

78

# Tunic

STITCHES: 1. Diagonal Mosaic
2. Parisian
3. Horizontal Double Brick
4. Hungarian
5. Double Brick
6. Horizontal Milanese
7. Basketweave

CANVAS: Interlock Mono 14, 3½″ × 13½″

YARN: Persian

NEEDLE: Size 20

SIZE OF FINISHED PROJECT: 3½″ × 13½″

Draw your name on a piece of paper and transfer the design to the canvas.

Should you need to add stitches, be careful not to choose any that distort the canvas.

Line the reverse side of your stitching.

Remember that if you stitch with wool yarn, you will always need to wash the garment in cold water or have it dry cleaned.

**Fig. 5-4a** *Tunic*

**Fig. 5-4b**

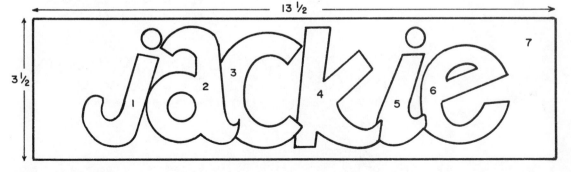

**Fig. 5-4c** *Close-up*

**Fig. 5-4d** *Alphabet*

ABCDEFGHI
JKLMNOPQR
STUVWXYZ
abcdefghijkl
mnopqrstuvwx
yz

*MAKING SOMETHING FROM NOTHING*

# Tooth fairy pillow

STITCHES:
1. Brick
2. Couching
3. Basketweave
4. French Knot
5. Straight
6. Hungarian

CANVAS:   Regular Mono 18 (Congress Cloth), 10″ × 10″ (1″ margins included); fabric for pocket

YARN:   Linen (initials); pearl cotton (face and hands), rayon floss (hair), velvet (wings and dress), metallic (trim and wand), and embroidery floss (tooth)

NEEDLE:   Size 20

SIZE OF FINISHED PROJECT:   8″ × 8″

Transfer the design to the canvas and stitch. Use a waste knot for the rayon floss (see page 28).

Cut two pieces of lightweight fabric for the pocket (see Figure 5–5c). Stitch along the seam line, leaving a small hole at the bottom. Trim the seam and turn the pocket inside out. Close the hole. Sew the pocket to the canvas.

Block (see page 157) and make into a pillow (see page 169).

**Fig. 5-5a**  *Tooth Fairy Pillow*

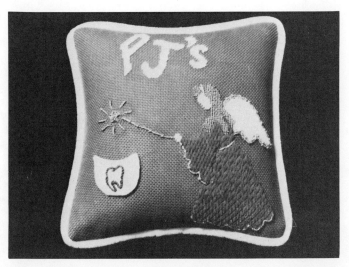

_PJ'S_

**Fig. 5-5b**

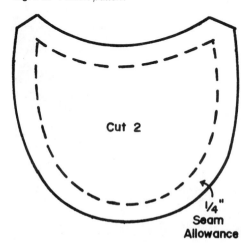

**Fig. 5-5c** _Pocket pattern_

Cut 2

1/4"
Seam
Allowance

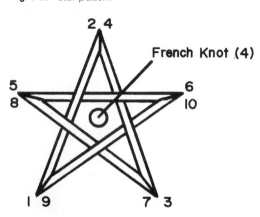

**Fig. 5-5d** _Star pattern_

2 4

French Knot (4)

5
8

6
10

1 9       7 3

*MAKING SOMETHING FROM NOTHING*

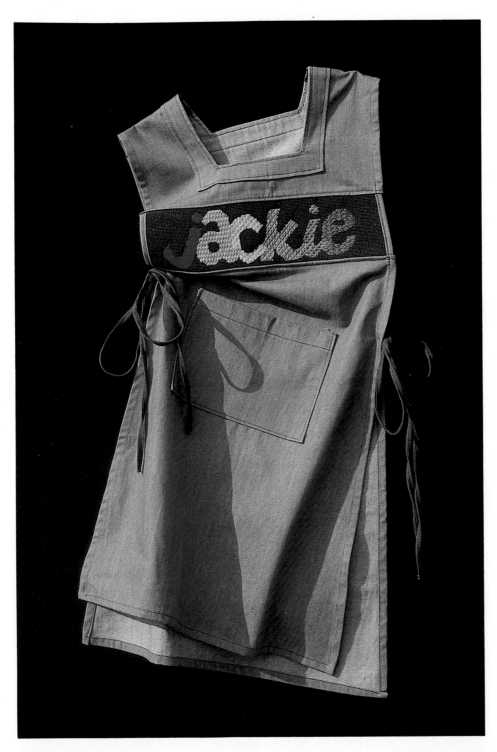

PLATE 1. Tunic.
Designed by the author and stitched by Jackie Beaty.

PLATE 2 *(below)*. Briefcase.
Designed and stitched by the author.

PLATE 3 *(bottom left)*. Card Case.
Designed and stitched by the author.

PLATE 4 *(bottom right)*. Sampler Pillow.
Designed and stitched by Jackie Beaty.

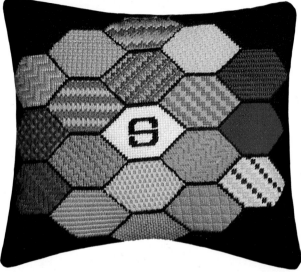

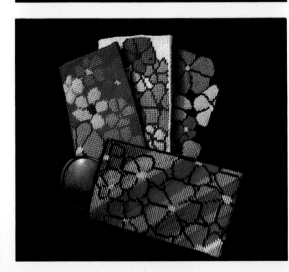

PLATE 5 *(top left)*. Vase of Flowers.
Designed and stitched by
Willard Lockett.

PLATE 6 *(top right)*. *TV Guide* Cover.
Designed and stitched by the author.

PLATE 7 *(center left)*. Strawberries.
Designed and stitched by
Mickey McKitrick.

PLATE 8 *(center right)*. Rainbow Case.
Designed and stitched by the author.

PLATE 9 *(left)*. Flower Eyeglass Cases.
Designed and stitched by
Barbara Johnston.

PLATE 10. Mouse and Cheese.
Designed by the author
and stitched by Mary Savage.

PLATE 11. Crayon Box.
Designed and stitched by the author.

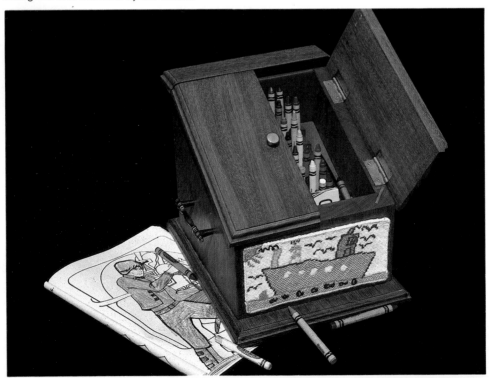

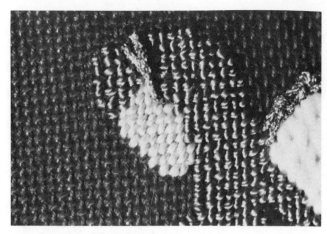

**Fig. 5-5e** *Close-up*

# Card case

STITCHES:  1. Continental
2. Basketweave (where possible)

CANVAS:  Interlock Mono 12, 2¾″ × 4¾″

YARN:  Persian

NEEDLE:  Size 20

SIZE OF FINISHED PROJECT:  4½″ × 6¼″ × 1″

The myriad of colors in this project will make a neat back difficult. Take care not to pull the yarn too tightly. Excess tension will distort this design. The included iron-on lining helps to hold it in place.

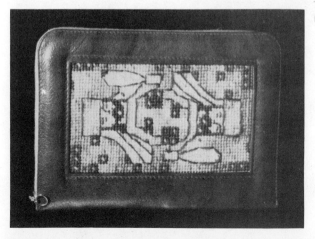

**Fig. 5-6a** *Card Case*

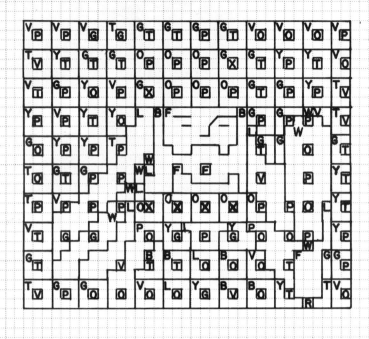

**Fig. 5-6b** *Graph chart*

**Fig. 5-6d** *Close-up*

**Fig. 5-6c**

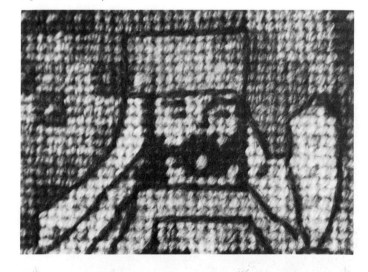

*MAKING SOMETHING FROM NOTHING*

# Jewelry box

STITCHES:
1. Mosaic
2. Basketweave
3. Continental
4. Irregular Continental
5. Running Stitch (pink pads on octopus's tentacles
6. Chain
7. Twisted Chain
8. Couching
9. Raised Buttonhole on Raised Band
10. French Knots

CANVAS: Penelope or Mono 10, 12½″ × 22½″ (3″ margins included)

YARN: Persian, tapestry, linen (octopus's tentacles), rayon floss (fish), metallic (trunk trim and jewelry)

NEEDLE: Size 20

SIZE OF FINISHED PROJECT: 6½″ × 16½″

The shading technique used in the water and the sand is a good way to use scraps to cover a large area—and it gives a wonderful effect of depth to both areas. The Irregular Continental Stitch fits in perfectly.

I used 5–7 different blues and 5–7 different browns. I grabbed one strand and stitched until it was gone. I then stitched with another color until it was gone—and so on.

The Chain Stitch, Twisted Chain, and Couching Stitch were placed on top of the background (except for the fish).

The Irregular Continental distorts the canvas *horribly!* Blocking (see page 157) should be done twice—once to get it generally straight and a second time to strive for perfection. The 3″ margins are necessary for a big blocking job.

*DO NOT* put the Couching Stitch on the canvas until after it has been blocked twice. Otherwise the stitch will be crooked.

Mount the needlepoint on a piece of plywood according to the directions on page 168. Insert the finished panel into or onto a box lid or into a picture frame. Glue rhinestones in place.

**Fig. 5-7a** *Jewelry Box*

**Fig. 5-7b** *Chart*

**Fig. 5-7c**
*Close-up*

PART THREE
# THE STITCHES

Before you even start to stitch, you will need to know the definitions of the symbols used in the drawings. The artist's signature  shows the location of the beginning of the stitch. In stitches that are done in steps, the starts are identified by $\mathcal{O}_1$, $\mathcal{O}_A$, $\mathcal{O}_a$, $\mathcal{O}_{AA}$ and $\mathcal{O}$ aa, in that order.

Arrows alone indicate a row change with no turning of the canvas. Arrows accompanied by a clock show a turning of the canvas:

T ⟳ means, "Turn 90° to the right."

T ⟱ means, "Turn 180°."

T ↵ means, "Turn 90° to the left."

Where they would complicate things, these arrows and clocks have been omitted. But you can still tell where to turn the canvas. Simply turn the book so that the numbers are upright. Turn your canvas the same way and stitch.

When several stitches go into the same hole, the numbers have been omitted because there simply is not room for all of them (see Chapter 10 on Eye Stitches).

The numbering has been arranged to create the best possible backing. Economical use of yarn usually creates a poor backing, which reduces the durability of a needlepoint piece.

A change of color is indicated by darkening the stitches, but the use of a second color is not absolutely necessary. This darkening also helps you to see the next row more clearly. Other colors (third, fourth, etc.) are indicated by different designs within each stitch. When working with two colors that cross each other, put the darker color on the bottom. Work the lighter colors last.

The canvas pictured is the canvas used for the particular stitch. Generally, all stitches can be worked on Penelope canvas; Regular Mono canvas does have some restrictions on types of stitches that can be used. These stitches have been pictured on Penelope canvas. The rest of the stitches have been drawn on Mono canvas for simplicity and clarity.

# Chapter six

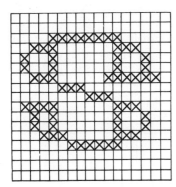

# STRAIGHT STITCHES

## Straight stitches

Straight Stitches are those stitches that cover the canvas vertically or horizontally. A vertical stitch covers two to six horizontal mesh and lies entirely between two vertical mesh. A horizontal stitch covers two to six vertical mesh and lies entirely between two horizontal mesh.

A single strand of both tapestry and Persian yarn, when worked in Straight Stitches, covers Mono 14 canvas well. On Penelope or Mono 10 or 12 you will have to thicken your yarn.

Straight Stitches make beautiful patterns, and they also make a good background (as a rule). They work up quickly and can give a good backing if you plan on it.

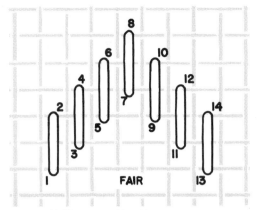

**Fig. 6-a** *Making a good backing*

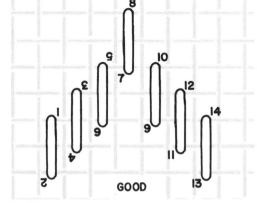

**Fig. 6-b**

Straight Stitches do not distort the canvas when you stitch. I recommend Straight Stitches for beginners.

Take a Bargello tuck as you bury the tail (see page 28).

If you wish to mix Straight Stitches with Diagonal Stitches, you can refer to page 32 for directions.

| STRAIGHT STITCHES | Border | Good Backing | Poor Backing | Background | Design | Accent | Fast | Slow | Geometric Pattern | Shading | Yarn Hog | Snags | Snag-Proof | Little Texture | Medium Texture | High Relief | Flower Stitch | Weak Pattern | Medium Pattern | Strong Pattern | Distorts Canvas |
|---|---|---|---|---|---|---|---|---|---|---|---|---|---|---|---|---|---|---|---|---|---|
| Straight Gobelin | • | • | | • | • | | | | • | | | | • | • | | | | • | | | |
| Split Gobelin | | • | | • | • | | | • | | • | • | | • | • | | | | • | ' | | |
| Straight Stitch | | | | | | | | | | | | | | | | | | | | | |
| Brick | | • | | • | • | | | | • | • | | | • | • | | | | • | | | |
| Giant Brick | | • | | • | • | | • | | • | • | | • | | • | | | | | • | | |
| Double Brick | | • | | • | • | | • | | • | | | | | • | | | | | • | | |
| Horizontal Brick | | • | | • | • | | • | | • | • | | • | | • | | | | | • | | |
| Parisian | | • | | • | • | | • | | • | • | | | | • | | | | | • | | |
| Pavillion | • | • | | • | • | | • | | • | | | | | • | | | | | • | | |
| Hungarian | • | • | | • | • | • | • | | • | | | | | • | | | | | • | | |
| Horizontal Old Florentine | | • | | • | • | | • | | • | | | • | | • | | | | | • | | |
| Horizontal Milanese | | • | | • | • | • | • | | • | | | • | | • | | | | | | | • |

# Straight Gobelin

This stitch can be worked over any number of mesh, up to six.

**Fig. 6-1a**

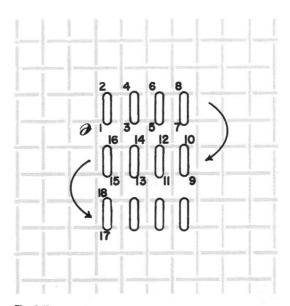

**Fig. 6-1b**

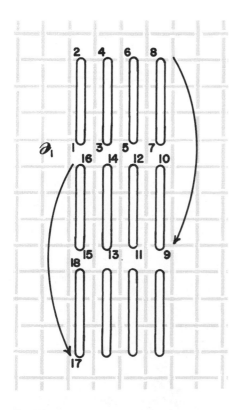

**Fig. 6-1c**

## Split gobelin

This stitch is based on embroidery's Split Stitch. It is particularly good for shading. Work this stitch over 2 to 5 mesh.

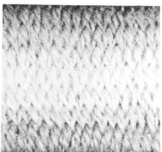

**Fig. 6-2a**

**Fig. 6-2b**

## Straight stitch

I've used this term to indicate any stitch that is taken by placing thread or yarn between point A and point B. It may take several stitches, laid side by side, to fill the area (actually Satin Stitch), or it may take several stitches in different directions to create the desired effect.

**Fig. 6-3a**

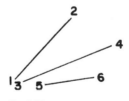

**Fig. 6-3b**

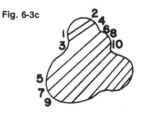

**Fig. 6-3c**

# Brick

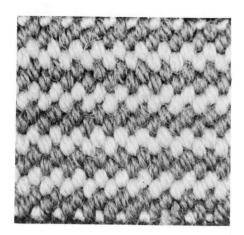

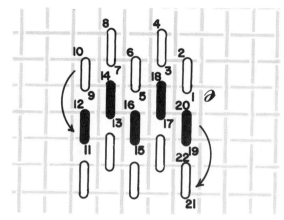

Fig. 6-4a      Fig. 6-4b

# Giant brick

This stitch may be worked over four or six mesh with an even step.

Fig. 6-5a      Fig. 6-5b

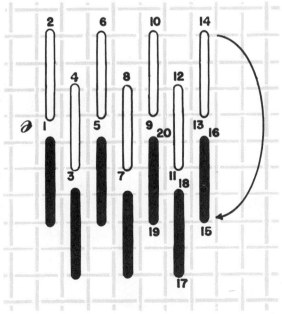

# Double brick

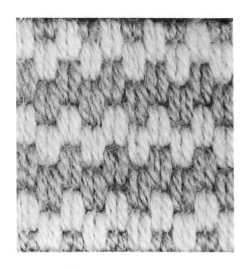

Fig. 6-6a

Fig. 6-6b

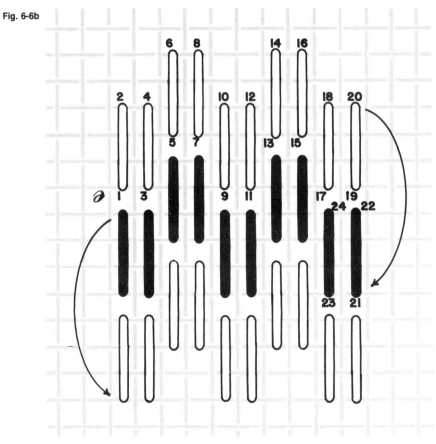

# Horizontal brick

This stitch can be worked over two or four mesh.

Fig. 6-7a

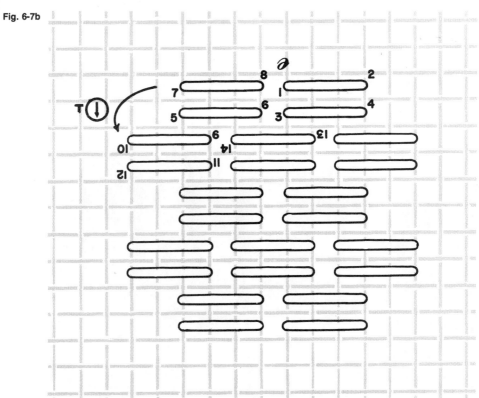

Fig. 6-7b

Parisian is a combination of long and short stitches (over two and four mesh). The tall stitches are over the short stitches.

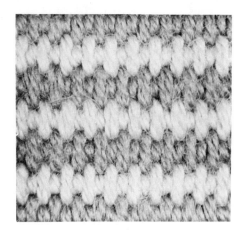

**Fig. 6-8a**

**Fig. 6-8b**

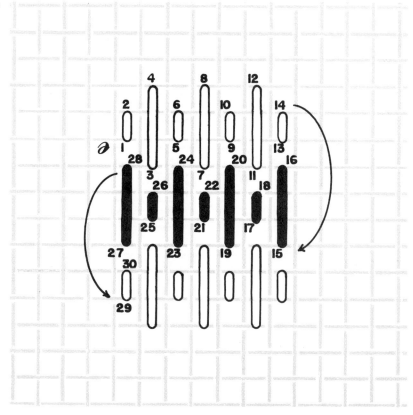

The diamonds share the short stitch.

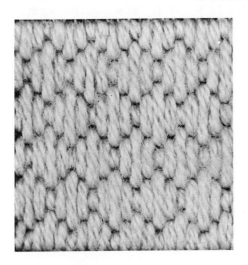

Fig. 6-9a

Fig. 6-9b

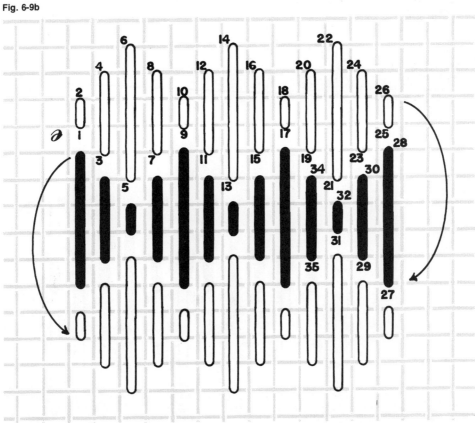

This vertical stitch establishes a diamond pattern. It is good in two colors, although it is stunning in one color. It is a set of three stitches—2:4:2. Skip a space. Repeat 2:4:2. Skip a space under the long stitch. Continue the pattern—2:4:2, then skip, then 2:4:2, and so on.

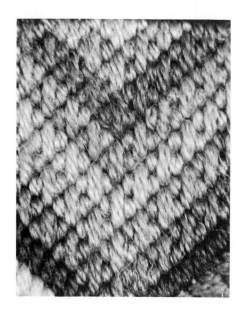

**Fig. 6-10a**

**Fig. 6-10b**

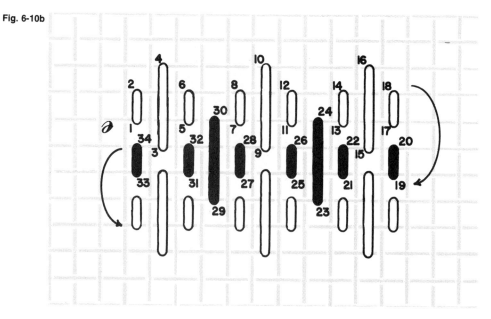

# Horizontal old florentine

When all the short stitches are worked in a second color, the stitch resembles a woven basket.

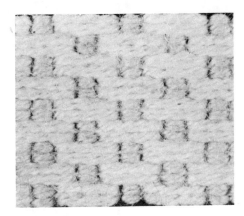

**Fig. 6-11a**

**Fig. 6-11b**

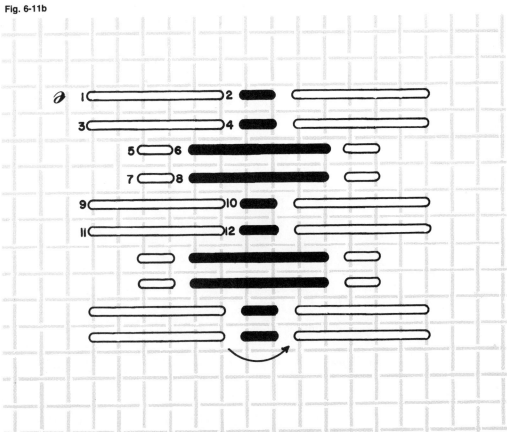

# Horizontal milanese

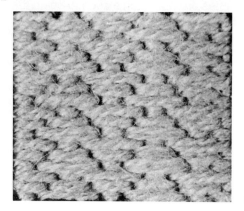

**Fig. 6-12**

# Chapter seven

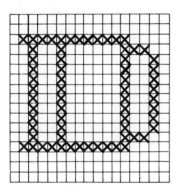

# IAGONAL STITCHES

## Diagonal stitches

Diagonal Stitches cover the canvas by crossing junctions of mesh rather than going between them. In referring to these slanted stitches, I have designated the angle or slant they take by two numbers. The first number refers to the number of mesh that you go up or down. The second number refers to the number of mesh that you go over. For example, a 1 × 1 stitch is a Tent Stitch; a 1 × 3 stitch is shown in Figures a and b; 3 × 1 and 3 × 3 stitches are shown in Figures c, d, and e. For those stitches where both numbers are the same, you may count, diagonally, the junctions of mesh instead of counting up three and over three. Whether you go up or down (for the first number) is shown in the sketch that accompanies each stitch.

Mono or Penelope 10 canvas usually accepts one strand of tapestry or Persian yarn for Diagonal Stitches.

Tent Stitches are Basketweave, Continental, and Half-Cross.

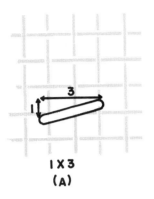

**I X 3**
**(A)**

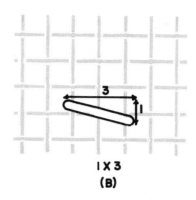

**I X 3**
**(B)**

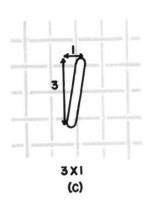

**3 X I**
**(C)**

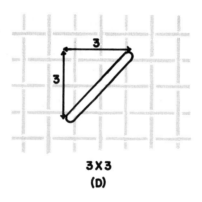

**3 X 3**
**(D)**

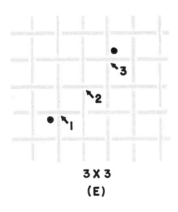

**3 X 3**
**(E)**

**Fig. 7 a-e**  *How to read Diagonal Stitch Diagrams*

*THE STITCHES*

# DIAGONAL STITCHES

| Stitch | Border | Good Backing | Poor Backing | Background | Design | Accent | Fast | Slow | Geometric Pattern | Shading | Yarn Hog | Snags | Snag-Proof | Little Texture | Medium Texture | High Relief | Flower Stitch | Weak Pattern | Medium Pattern | Strong Pattern | Distorts Canvas |
|---|---|---|---|---|---|---|---|---|---|---|---|---|---|---|---|---|---|---|---|---|---|
| Basketweave | | • | | • | • | | | | | | | | • | • | | | | • | | | |
| Continental | | • | | | • | | | | | • | | | • | • | | | | • | | | • |
| Half-Cross | | | • | | | | | | | | | | • | • | | | | • | | | • |
| Irregular Continental | | • | | • | • | | | | | | | | | • | | | | | • | | • |
| Slanted Gobelin | | • | | • | • | | • | | • | • | | • | | • | | | | | • | | • |
| Lazy Kalem | | • | | • | • | | | | | | | | • | • | | | | • | | | |
| Byzantine #1 | | • | | • | • | | • | | | • | | • | | • | | | | | | • | • |
| Jacquard | | • | | • | • | | | | | | | | | • | | | | | | • | • |
| Diagonal Hungarian Ground | | • | | • | • | | • | | | | | | | • | | | | | | • | • |
| Milanese | | • | | • | • | • | | | | | | • | | | • | | | | | • | • |
| Oriental | | • | | • | • | • | | | | | | • | | • | | | | | | • | • |

Basketweave is one of the most used and misused stitches in needlepoint. It is an excellent stitch to know and to use. A durable backing, resembling a woven pattern, is created. This makes it a "must" for chairs, footstools, and other items that will receive lots of wear.

The finished piece is not distorted, but it still needs blocking (see page 157). Basketweave allows a worked canvas to give a lot yet still be strong. It can be worked without turning the canvas. Because it lacks maneuverability, it is not a good stitch for designing. (Use Continental for designing in very small areas if you want a Tent Stitch.)

Study Figure 7–1. Note that, basically, the stitch fills the canvas in diagonal rows, starting at the upper right corner.

As you work you will notice that a pattern is developing. In making an up row, the needle always goes straight across under two mesh. In making a down row, the needle always goes straight down under two mesh. Notice that the first of these two mesh is covered by a stitch in the preceding row. It is a very common error to go across or under these mesh by not counting the covered one.

At the end of each row there is what many students refer to as a turn stitch. Actually it is the first stitch of a new row. If it helps you to consider it a turn stitch, then do so. At the end of the up row this is a horizontal Continental Stitch, and at the end of the down row this is a vertical Continental Stitch. The common error here is to leave the turn stitch out. Often students get carried away and make two turn stitches. If you think that you have made an error somewhere, check to see if this is it.

When your yarn runs out and you must start another one, be sure to start *exactly* where you left off. If you do not, a line will show on the right side. For example, if your yarn runs out at the end of an up row, do not start the new yarn at the bottom of that up row you just finished, thus starting another up row. Instead, you should be at the top of that last up row, ready to begin a down row. Most people tend to put their work away for the day when they have finished working the yarn on the needle. It might help you not to do this when working Basketweave. Leave the needle threaded with half a yarn and stick it into the canvas in position ready to take the next stitch. This way you will not lose your place.

When working Basketweave on Regular Mono canvas, note that at the intersections of mesh in a horizontal row, the vertical mesh alternate between being on top of and underneath the horizontal mesh. However, on the diagonal, the vertical mesh are always on top or underneath the horizontal mesh.

If you will take care always to cover the vertical mesh intersections with a down row and to cover the horizontal mesh intersections with an up row, you will produce a stitch that is very even in appearance on the right side. This will also help you to keep track of up rows and down rows (see preceding discussion).

When you come to the end of each strand of yarn, weave it under the yarns on the back side of the canvas for about an inch. Follow the weave that the stitch makes. Clip it closely to keep the back neat. If you work the beginning and ending tails under any other way, a ridge will form that will show on the right side.

Basketweave is not frightfully complicated. It may take some study on your part, but once you get the hang of the stitch you will enjoy working it. It has a certain rhythm that develops easily. You can achieve a perfection with this stitch that is unique. Use it no matter how small the area. (When the area is absolutely too small and when outlining, use the Continental Stitch.)

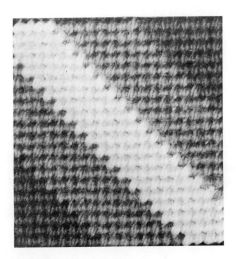

Fig. 7-1a

**Fig. 7-1b**

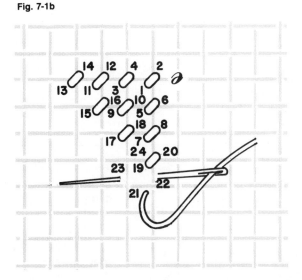

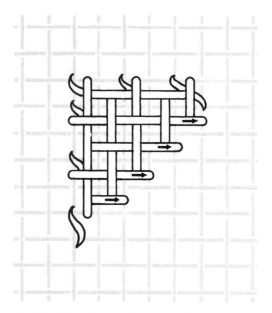

**Fig. 7-1c** *Basketweave: Sequence of stitches*

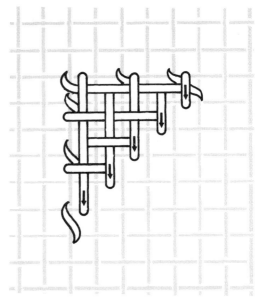

**Fig. 7-1d** *Basketweave: Wrong side—last row is down row (top); last row is up row (bottom)*

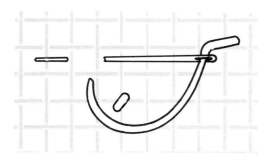

**Fig. 7-1e** *Basketweave: Right—up row covering a horizontal mesh intersection*

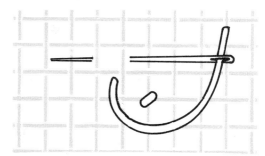

**Fig. 7-1f** *Basketweave: Wrong—up row covering a vertical mesh intersection*

## Continental

The Continental Stitch forms the next best backing after Basketweave, and it is the next most distinct stitch of the Tent Stitches. Its main drawback is that it pulls the canvas badly out of shape.

You really should use Basketweave wherever you can. But Continental will get the very small areas that Basketweave cannot.

If you insist on using Continental instead of Basketweave, you should try to make the stitches as even and
uniform as possible. You may work Continental either horizontally or vertically. Choose the direction that best fills the
area you have. Work the stitch in that direction for the whole
space. Combinations of horizontally and vertically worked
Continental will produce lines on the right side. Always work
this stitch from right to left. If you are filling a large space, do
not turn the canvas upside down for the second row; cut the
yarn and begin the second row below the first on the right.
Figure 7–2 does not show this because I do not recommend
that you use this stitch in a large enough area to matter.

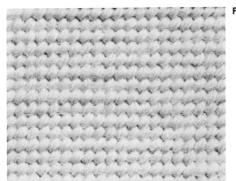

**Fig. 7-2a**

**Fig. 7-2b**  *Continental: Horizontal—work left to right*

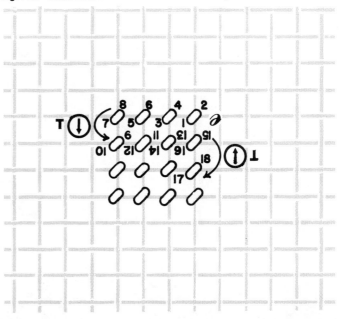

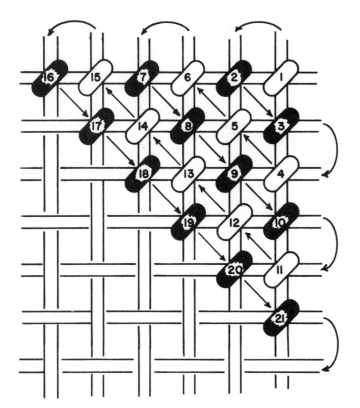

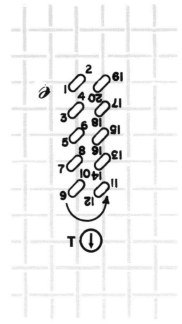

**Fig. 7-2c** *Continental: Vertical—work down*

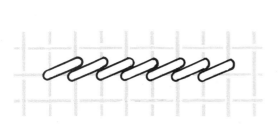

**Fig. 7-2d** *Continental: Reverse Side*

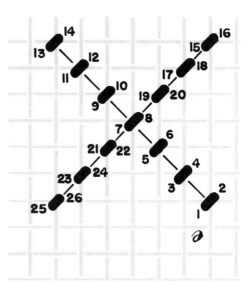

**Fig. 7-2e** *Continental: Outlining*

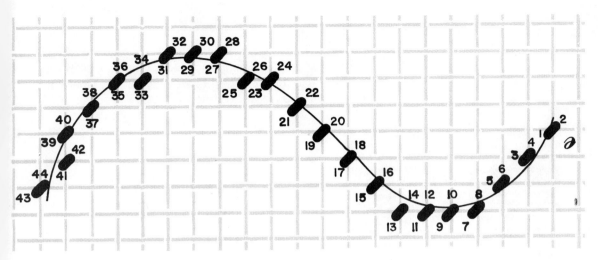

**Fig. 7-2f** *Continental: Outlining*

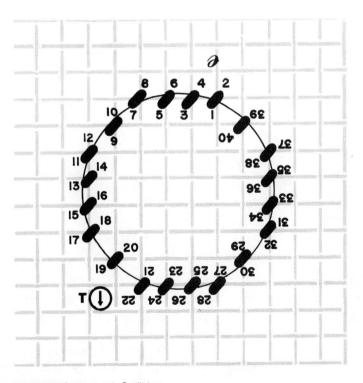

**Fig. 7-2g** *Continental: Outlining*

## Half-Cross

The Half-Cross Stitch produces the poorest backing of the Tent Stitches, and the stitch is not distinct. I do not allow my students to use this stitch, and I strongly suggest that you replace it with Basketweave and Continental.

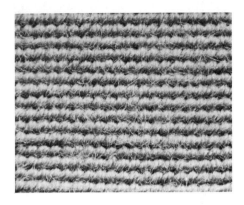

**Fig. 7-3a**

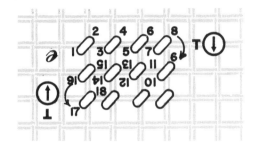

**Fig. 7-3b**  *Half Cross: Reverse side*

**Fig. 7-3c**  *Half Cross: Horizontal*

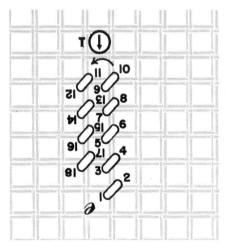

**Fig. 7-3d**  *Half Cross: Vertical*

## Irregular continental

This stitch is excellent for shading. In working it, be sure to keep it a 1 × 1, 2 × 2, 3 × 3, 4 × 4, or 5 × 5 stitch. Count the mesh junctions diagonally (see page 102). The rows will be irregular. Figure 7–4 is an example only. Do your own. Take a Bargello tuck when you bury the tails (see page 28).

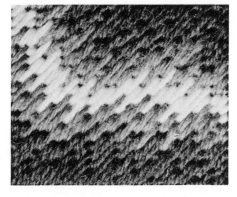

Fig. 7-4

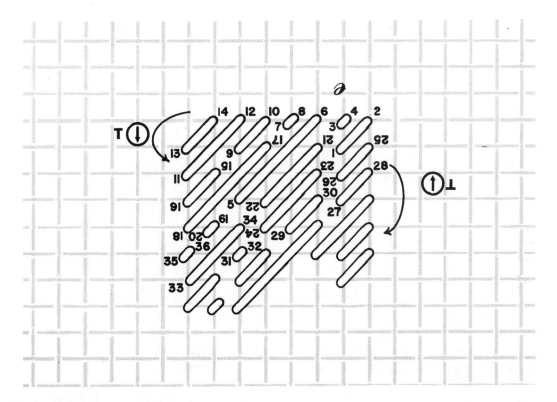

# Slanted gobelin

This stitch is versatile, for it can be worked between two and six mesh tall and one or two mesh wide. When the stitch is taller than two mesh, you will probably need to thicken your yarn.

Slanted Gobelin makes a horizontal row. It is good for dresser drawers or anything else in rows.

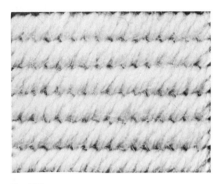
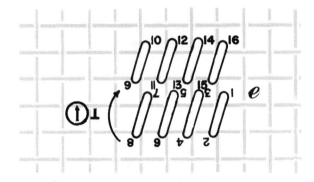

**Fig. 7-5**

# Lazy kalem

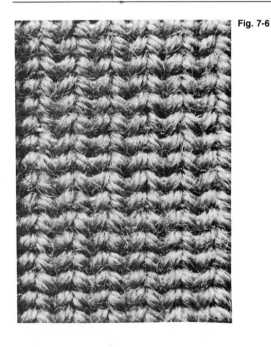

**Fig. 7-6**

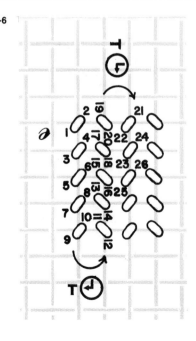

# Byzantine

Byzantine makes good steps and fills in diagonally shaped areas well. Take a Bargello tuck as you bury the tails (see page 28).

**Fig. 7-7**

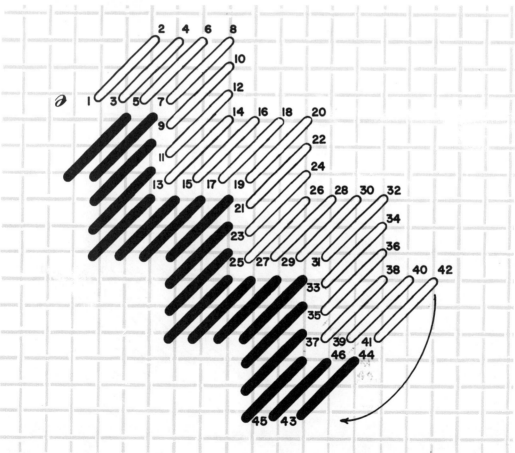

# Jacquard

Jacquard is very much like the Byzantine Stitch with a Continental Stitch divider.

Fig. 7-8

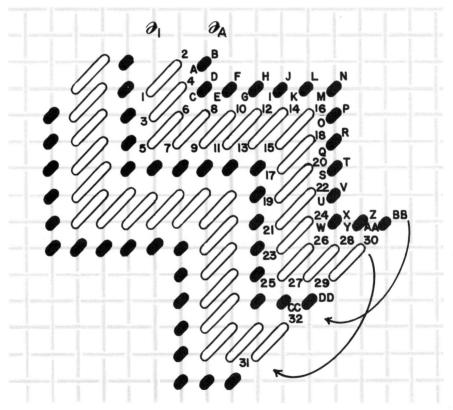

# Diagonal hungarian ground

Work this stitch in two colors or work a very large, uninterrupted area in one color; otherwise, the pattern is lost.

Fig. 7-9

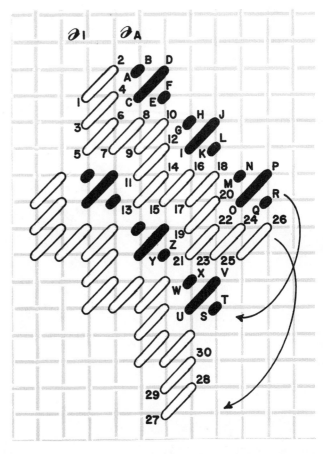

This is an especially pretty stitch, but it is difficult to work around lots of letters.

**Fig. 7-10**

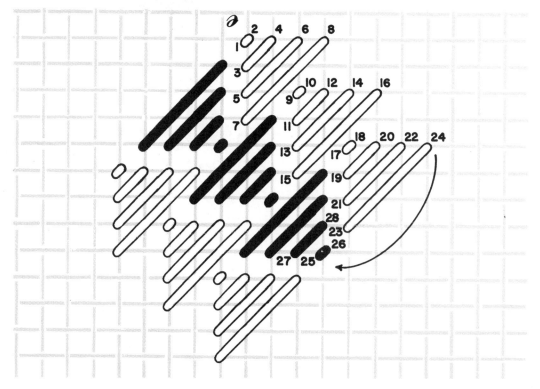

*THE STITCHES*

The Oriental Stitch makes a good background in one color. It looks entirely different in two colors. Few stitches undergo such a change in appearance. Try it both ways.

**Fig. 7-11**

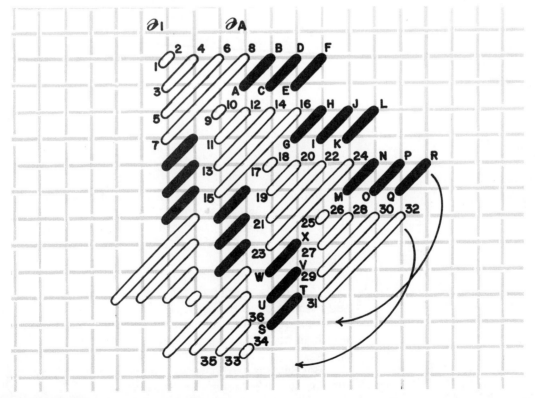

# Chapter eight

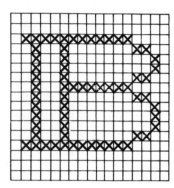OX STITCHES

## Box stitches

Box stitches are a series of diagonal stitches that form squares or boxes. The Diagonal Box Stitches are simply boxes laid in a diagonal line, with the corners overlapping. (See the Diagonal Cashmere Stitch). Note how the short stitch is shared.

Most of these stitches make excellent borders. They lend themselves to beautiful geometric patterns in several colors. I have gone into only a few color variations, for there are whole books that discuss color variations of just a few stitches.

Box Stitches can be worked on Penelope 10 or Mono 10 with one strand of tapestry or Persian yarn.

Box Stitches almost always distort the canvas. However, reversing the boxes corrects this problem. Don't let a mistake slide—an error will stick out like a sore thumb because the pattern is more precise than in other stitches. Double check your work every few rows.

All Box Stitches can be used in designing, and many are good for background. Almost all produce a geometric pattern, and all form a good backing, which means that your finished piece will wear well.

| BOX STITCHES | Border | Good Backing | Poor Backing | Background | Design | Accent | Fast | Slow | Geometric Pattern | Shading | Yarn Hog | Snags | Snag-Proof | Little Texture | Medium Texture | High Relief | Flower Stitch | Weak Pattern | Medium Pattern | Strong Pattern | Distorts Canvas |
|---|---|---|---|---|---|---|---|---|---|---|---|---|---|---|---|---|---|---|---|---|---|
| Mosaic | • | • | | • | • | | • | | • | | | | • | • | | | | • | | | • |
| Reversed Mosaic | • | • | | • | • | | • | | • | | | | • | • | | | | • | | | |
| Diagonal Mosaic | | • | | • | • | | • | | • | • | | | • | • | | | | • | | | • |
| Cashmere | • | • | | • | • | | • | | • | | | | • | • | | | | • | | | • |
| Reversed Cashmere | | | | | | | | | | | | | | | | | | | | | |
| Diagonal Cashmere | | • | | • | • | | • | | • | • | | | • | • | | | | | • | • | • |
| Scotch | • | • | | • | • | | • | | • | | | | | • | | | | • | | | |
| Woven Scotch | | | | | | | | | | | | | | | | | | | | | |
| Reversed Scotch | • | • | | • | • | | • | | • | | | | | • | | | | • | | | |
| Moorish Stitch | | • | | • | • | | • | | • | | | | | • | | | | | | • | • |

## Mosaic

Mosaic is the smallest of the Box Stitches. It is just three diagonal stitches: short, long, short. It makes a box two by two mesh. Mosaic is an excellent background or design stitch. This stitch is a good background to work behind Continental letters. It can be worked horizontally, vertically, or diagonally.

Fig. 8-1a

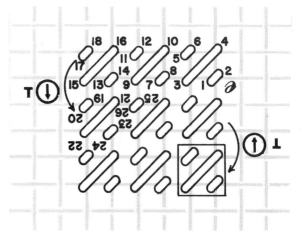

**Fig. 8-1b**  *Mosaic: Horizontal*

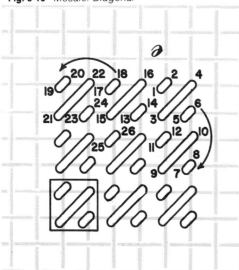

**Fig. 8-1c**  *Mosaic: Diagonal*

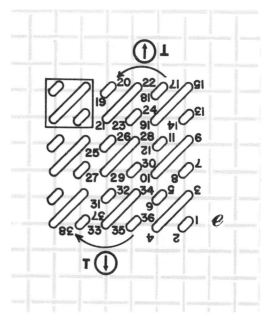

**Fig. 8-1d**  *Mosaic: Vertical*

# Reversed mosaic

This stitch is worked most easily by doing a diagonal row from upper left to lower right. Then turn the canvas 90° so that the upper right now becomes the upper left. Work the same type of diagonal row, filling in the blank spaces. I think this stitch looks best in one color.

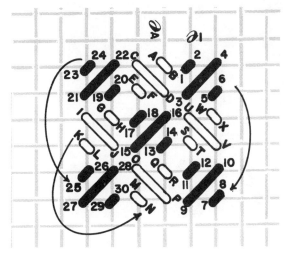

**Fig. 8-2**

# Diagonal mosaic

When Mosaic is worked diagonally, it becomes merely a line of short and long stitches. For this reason, you may use it for shading. Do this stitch in one or more colors.

**Fig. 8-3**

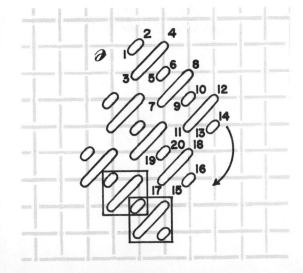

Cashmere is a rectangular Mosaic Stitch. It can be worked horizontally, vertically, or diagonally.

Fig. 8-4

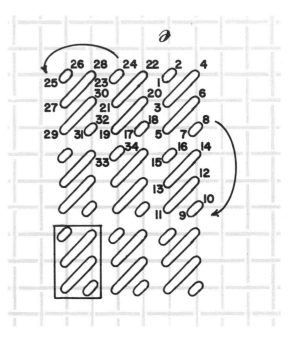

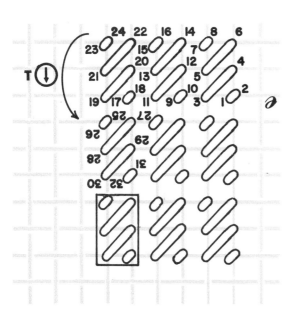

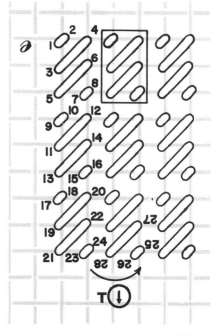

# Reversed cashmere

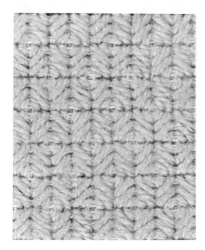

Work in diagonal rows. Turn the canvas 90° for the next row. Start with the widest part of the area to be filled.

**Fig. 8-5**

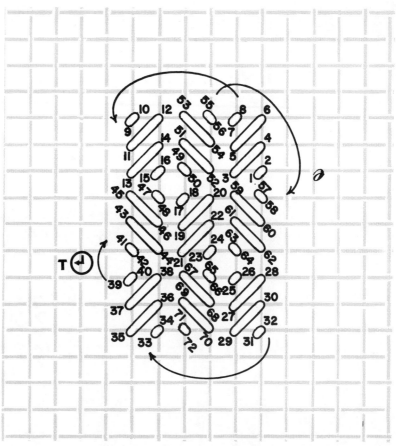

# Diagonal cashmere

The second row of Diagonal Cashmere is a bit tricky to work. I try to remember that the first long stitch in the second row is diagonally below the last short stitch. After I have taken that stitch, I go back and pick up the first short stitch in the second row.

**Fig. 8-6**

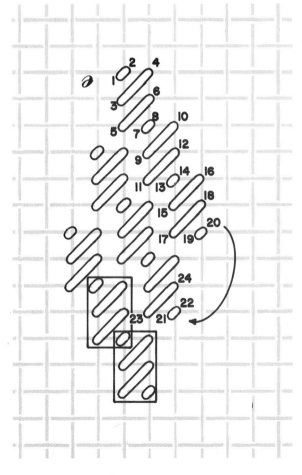

# Scotch

The Scotch Stitch is merely a large Mosaic Stitch. It has many lovely variations. This stitch can be worked three ways (see Mosaic and Cashmere Stitches).

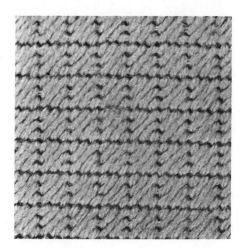

**Fig. 8-7**

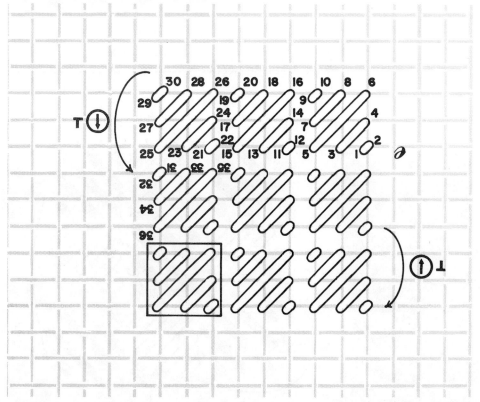

## Woven scotch

This stitch is worked like a regular Scotch Stitch, except that the contrasting color of yarn is woven under the first, third, and fifth stitches.

**Fig. 8-8**

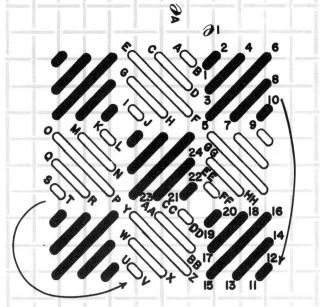

## Reversed scotch

Try this stitch in one color. See Reversed Mosaic for hints on working Reversed Scotch.

**Fig. 8-9**

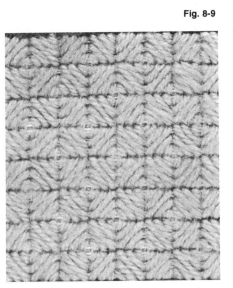

# Moorish

This is simply a Diagonal Scotch with a separating row of Continental Stitch. It resembles stairs; it can be used for rooftops and geometric designs.

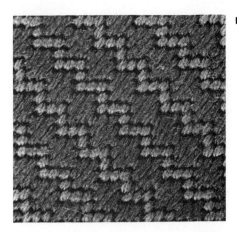

**Fig. 8-10**

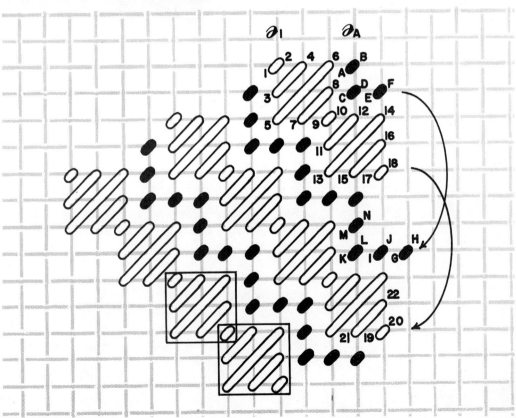

# Chapter nine

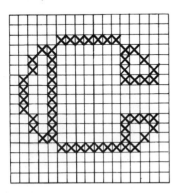ROSS
STITCHES

## Cross stitches

Cross Stitches make pretty filling, design, and border stitches. They often stand alone to represent flowers.

When working on Regular Mono canvas, the Cross Stitch must be crossed as you go. Watch the numbering as you go through this section.

It does not matter whether you cross the right arm over the left or the left arm over the right—but you must be consistent. I find it easier to work the whole area in half of the cross first. Then I go back and cross those stitches. I manage to ruin it every time if I don't do this.

Penelope 7 or 8 is ideal for Cross Stitches. Many of the

Cross Stitches do not need thickening; however, many do. When the Cross Stitch is worked on smaller canvas, it is not distinct. Larger crosses can be worked successfully on smaller canvas.

Cross Stitches come in varying sizes, so as a group they are quite versatile—you can use them for accent, for design, and for background. They also create some variety of texture. Many produce a geometric pattern.

| CROSS STITCHES | Border | Good Backing | Poor Backing | Background | Design | Accent | Fast | Slow | Geometric Pattern | Shading | Yarn Hog | Snags | Snag-Proof | Little Texture | Medium Texture | High Relief | Flower Stitch | Weak Pattern | Medium Pattern | Strong Pattern | Distorts Canvas |
|---|---|---|---|---|---|---|---|---|---|---|---|---|---|---|---|---|---|---|---|---|---|
| Cross Stitch | | | | • | • | | | | • | • | • | | • | • | | | | • | • | | |
| Three-Stitch Cross | | | | • | • | | | | • | • | | | • | | • | | • | | • | | |
| Giant Rice | • | | | • | • | • | | | • | • | | • | | • | | | • | | | • | |
| Oblong Cross | | | | • | • | | | | | • | | | | • | | | | • | • | | |
| 1 × 3 Spaced Cross Tramé | | | | • | • | | | | | • | | • | | | | | • | | | | |
| Hitched Cross | • | | | • | • | • | | | | • | | | | | • | • | | | • | | |
| Double Stitch | | | | • | • | | | | | • | | | | | | • | • | | • | | |
| Upright Cross | | | | • | • | | | | • | • | | | • | • | | | • | | | | |
| Long Upright Cross | | | | • | • | • | | | | • | | | | • | | | | | • | | |
| Fern | | | • | • | • | | • | | | • | | | | | • | | | | • | | |
| Binding Stitch | • | | | | | | | • | | | | | | • | | • | | | | • | |
| Greek | • | | • | • | • | | | | | | • | | | • | | | | | | • | |
| Smyrna Cross | • | | | • | • | • | | | | • | | | | | | • | • | | | • | |
| Reversed Smyrna Cross | • | | | • | • | • | | | | • | | | | | | • | • | | | • | |

# Cross stitch

On Mono canvas, each Cross must be crossed right away. It is faster, however, to work Penelope Cross. Both look alike.

Fig. 9-1a

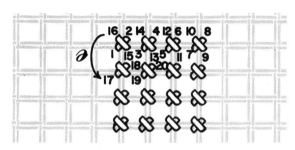

**Fig. 9-1b**  *Cross Stitch: Mono canvas*

**Fig. 9-1c**  *Cross Stitch: Penelope canvas*

# Three-stitch cross

You may need a tramé to cover the canvas.

Fig. 9-2

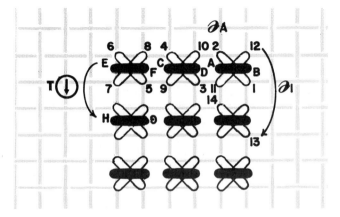

Take a Bargello tuck as you bury the tails (see page 28).

**Fig. 9-3**

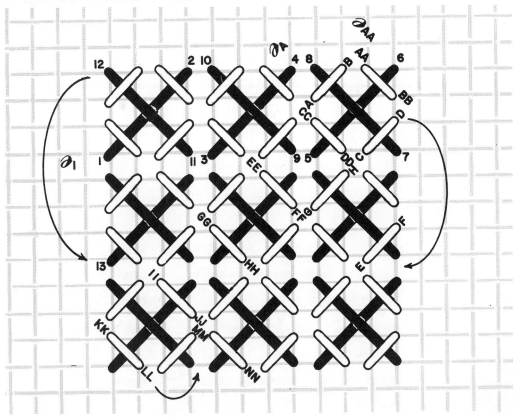

# Oblong cross

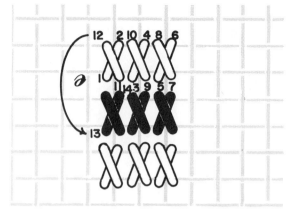

Fig. 9-4

## 1 × 3 Spaced cross tramé

This stitch is worked most easily by stitching a checkerboard pattern of Oblong Cross Stitches first and then by running a Tramé under them.

When the Tramé is worked in a dark shade of green and the Oblong Cross in a lighter shade of green, this stitch resembles grass.

The Tramé and Cross Stitches may run horizontally or vertically. Suit it to your needs.

Fig. 9-5

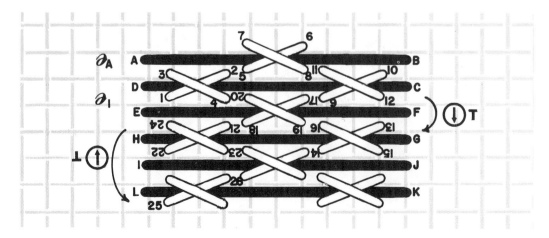

# Hitched cross

Fig. 9-6

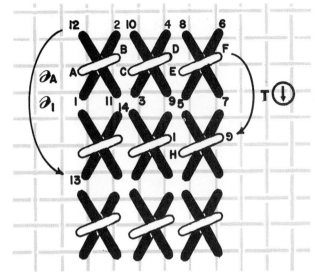

# Double stitch

This is a good stitch for creating a bumpy texture. When worked in one color it resembles tree bark. It is also good for polka dots.

Fig. 9-7

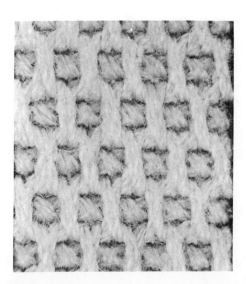

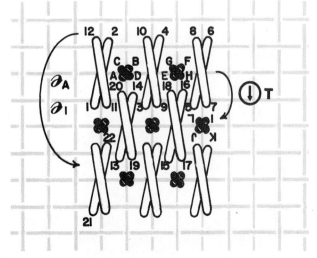

# Upright cross

Fig. 9-8

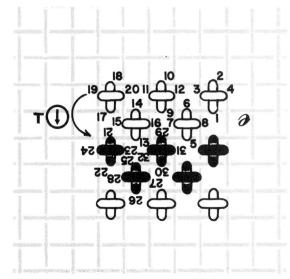

# Long upright cross

Fig. 9-9

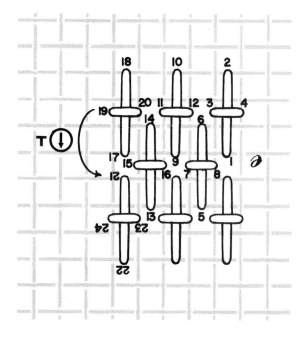

# Fern

Work this stitch in vertical columns from top to bottom only. Do not turn the canvas upside down for the next row. It makes a fat, neat braid. Fill the space at the top of the column with a Cross Stitch.

**Fig. 9-10**

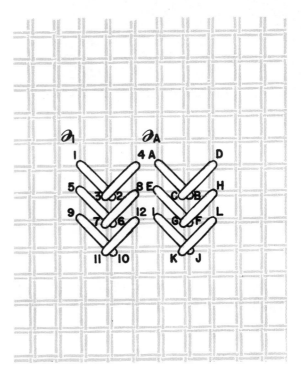

# Binding stitch

The Binding Stitch is not only useful, it is attractive, too. It finishes edges and sews seams (see page 28). It is worked only on the edges of canvas. You will need two threads of the canvas to secure it properly. On Penelope, this is one mesh; on Mono, two mesh.

Take a Bargello tuck as you bury the tails (see page 28).

The Binding Stitch is worked much like the Fern Stitch and it, too produces a braid.

Fig. 9-11a

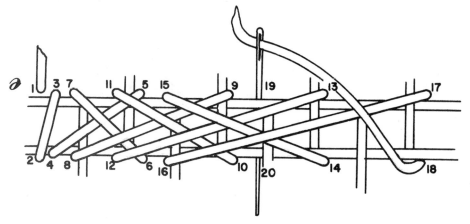

Fig. 9-11b

Fig. 9-11c  *Right*

**Fig. 9-11d**  *Wrong*

**Fig. 9-11e**  *Bottom half is fabric caught with the Binding Stitch*

## Greek

Work the Greek Stitch from left to right only. Break the yarn at the end of the row and begin again below the first stitch. It is actually a Cross Stitch with one short arm and one long arm. Each cross is intertwined with the next one.

**Fig. 9-12**

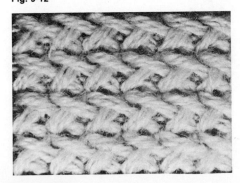

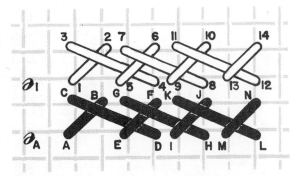

Make the X first, then the +. Smyrna Cross makes a good bump. When the + is worked in a light color, the stitch resembles hot cross buns. It is good for buttons, polka dots, and the like.

**Fig. 9-13**

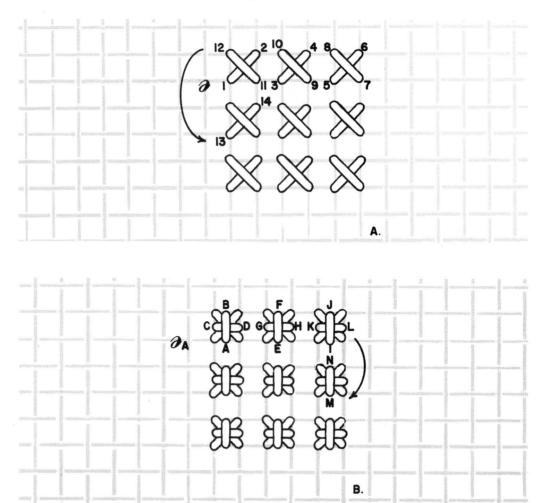

A.

B.

# Reversed smyrna crosses

**Fig. 9-14**

Chapter ten

# IED AND EYE STITCHES

## Tied stitches

The Tied Stitches are pretty, and many are good stitches for shading. The Periwinkle Stitch was especially designed to be accented with beads.

These stitches are somewhat slow, but most give good backings with little snagging on the right side of the canvas.

It is most important that you tie each stitch or group of stitches as you go. Each of the drawings is numbered; follow them closely.

The Tied Stitches are best worked on Mono 12 or 14 with a full strand of tapestry or Persian yarn.

The Tied Stitches are good for designs, and some can be used for background.

| TIED STITCHES | Border | Good Backing | Poor Backing | Background | Design | Accent | Fast | Slow | Geometric Pattern | Shading | Yarn Hog | Snags | Snag-Proof | Little Texture | Medium Texture | High Relief | Flower Stitch | Weak Pattern | Medium Pattern | Strong Pattern | Distorts Canvas |
|---|---|---|---|---|---|---|---|---|---|---|---|---|---|---|---|---|---|---|---|---|---|
| Couching | | • | | | • | • | • | | | | | • | | • | | | | • | | | |
| Web | | | | • | • | | • | | • | | | • | • | • | | | | • | | | |

## Couching

Couching is laying one yarn where you want it and tacking it down with another yarn. It curves well. Thread two needles. Try to tie at even intervals.

**Fig. 10-1**

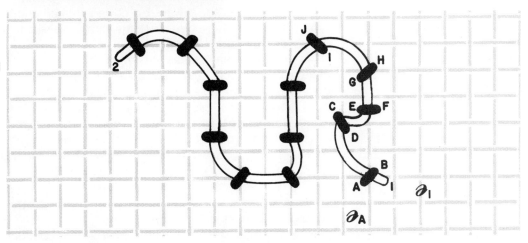

Fig. 10-2

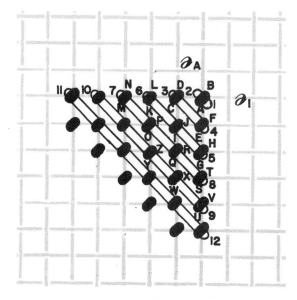

# Eye stitches

Eye Stitches are made by putting several stitches into one hole. This technique creates a hole, a dimple, or an eye.

Work Eye Stitches on Regular Mono 10. Use a full strand of tapestry or Persian yarn.

Eye Stitches are very pretty and interesting to do, but they are slow to work up. In stitching them, work from the outside to the center and always go down into the center. This will prevent splitting or snagging the yarn of the stitches you have already worked.

As you put what seems an impossible number of stitches into one small hole, take care that each of these stitches goes into the hole smoothly. If you are working on Regular Mono canvas, this task will be a little easier. It is a great help to enlarge the center hole by poking the point of a pair of embroidery scissors into it. Spread the mesh gently to enlarge the hole. This works only on Regular Mono (see Figure 10-3). Use 2-ply Persian yarn on other kinds.

You may need to pull the yarn more tightly as each eye forms. This helps to make the stitch smooth, but be careful not to pull the canvas out of shape.

Note that Eye Stitches usually begin with an Upright Cross, going from the outside into the center. Next, one stitch

**Fig. 10-3**

is taken in each quadrant in a circular motion until all the remaining stitches have been taken. The even-numbered stitches are all in the center of the eye, and because the numbers do not fit easily on the drawing, they have been omitted.

Eye Stitches lend themselves to broad borders, backgrounds, and pillows. Single motifs or clusters of two or three eyes make lovely flowers.

| EYE STITCHES | Border | Good Backing | Poor Backing | Background | Design | Accent | Fast | Slow | Geometric Pattern | Shading | Yarn Hog | Snags | Snag-Proof | Little Texture | Medium Texture | High Relief | Flower Stitch | Weak Pattern | Medium Pattern | Strong Pattern | Distorts Canvas |
|---|---|---|---|---|---|---|---|---|---|---|---|---|---|---|---|---|---|---|---|---|---|
| Ringed Daisies | • | • | | • | • | • | | • | • | | | | | | • | | • | | | • | |

# Ringed daisies

**Fig. 10-4**

Chapter eleven

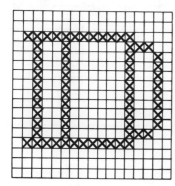

# ECORATIVE STITCHES

## Decorative stitches

These decorative stitches have many uses, some quite specialized and some more broad. They are not related in construction technique.

Most Decorative Stitches produce a poor backing and, therefore, are mostly used for accent. Many are poor choices for both design and background, so when using one of the Decorative Stitches, choose carefully.

| DECORATIVE STITCHES | Border | Good Backing | Poor Backing | Background | Design | Accent | Fast | Slow | Geometric Pattern | Shading | Yarn Hog | Snags | Snag-Proof | Little Texture | Medium Texture | High Relief | Flower Stitch | Weak Pattern | Medium Pattern | Strong Pattern | Distorts Canvas |
|---|---|---|---|---|---|---|---|---|---|---|---|---|---|---|---|---|---|---|---|---|---|
| Chain | • | | • | | • | • | | | | | | | • | | | | | | • | | |
| Twisted Chain | | | • | | • | | • | | | | • | | | | • | | | | • | | |
| Ridged Spider Web | | | • | | • | | • | | | • | | | | | • | • | | | | • | |
| French Knot | | | • | | • | | • | | | • | • | | | • | | • | | | • | | |
| Looped Turkey Work | | • | • | • | • | | | | • | • | • | | | | • | • | | | • | | |
| Cut Turkey Work | | • | • | • | • | | | | • | • | • | | | | • | • | • | | | | |
| Needleweaving | | | • | | • | • | | | | • | | | , | • | | • | | | | • | |
| Running Stitch | | | • | | • | • | • | | | | | | | • | | | | • | | | |
| Raised Buttonhole | | | • | • | | • | | • | | | | | | | • | | | • | | | |
| Raised Buttonhole on Raised Band | | | • | • | | | • | • | • | | | | | | • | | | • | | | |

## Chain

The Chain Stitch is quite a versatile stitch. It is one of a few stitches that curve. You may work it on top of the background or leave a space in the background to work the Chain Stitch.

This stitch is easier to work if you turn the canvas so that you are working horizontally and from right to left. Put on chain over 2 or 3 mesh.

**Fig. 11-1a**

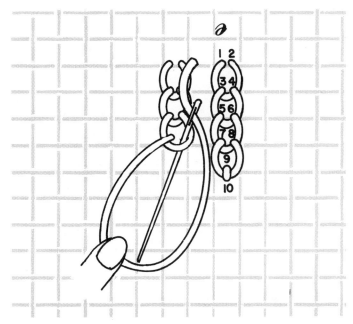

Fig. 11-1b

## Twisted chain

This stitch can be worked in a single row and curved to meet your purpose. It may also be worked side by side to fill an area. It is imperative that your tension be even. Work from top to bottom only.

Fig. 11-2

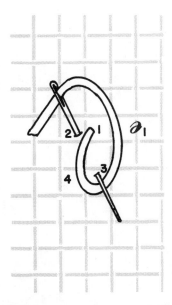

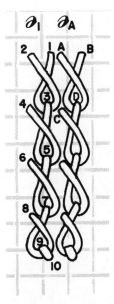

Bring the needle up as close to the center as you can without actually coming through the center. Go under two spokes and back over one; under two, over one. Do not penetrate the canvas until you are through. Keep going around and around until the spokes are no longer visible. When you think you cannot possibly get one more round in, do two more—then you are through!

To make a high ball, pull the yarn tight, but not so tightly that the spokes become misshapen. As you take each stitch, pull the yarn toward the center. This helps to tighten the stitch.

Use Spider Webs for grapes, apples, other fruits, wheels, balls, buttons, flowers, ladybugs, spiders, and other insects—anything round.

**Fig. 11-3**

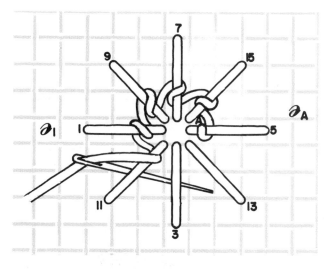

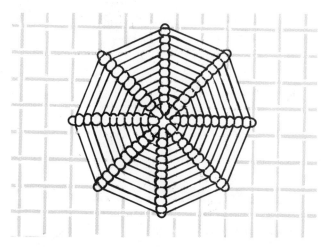

# French knot

French Knots are handy. They fill bare canvas and make polka dots, flower centers, whole flowers, and so forth.

**Fig. 11-4**

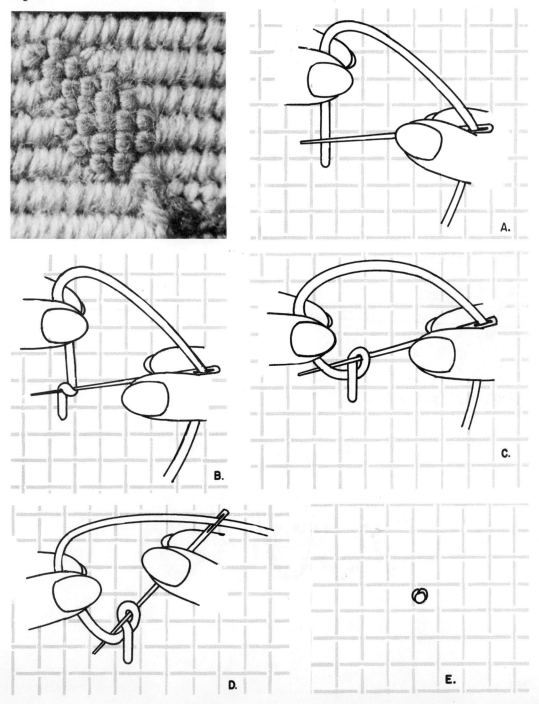

Stitch the bottom row first and work up. Work from left to right only. This means that you must cut your yarn at the end of every row. There is no tail to bury; it becomes part of the stitch. You may skip rows on a small canvas if it is too crowded.

Use a strip of paper to help you get the loops even (see Figures a, b, c). A drinking straw works well, too. In working Looped Turkey Work, try not to run out of yarn in the middle of a row unless you have to.

Turkey Work should be worked on an even number of mesh. However, when you get to the end of a row, there is often a mesh left over. Work the last three mesh by leaving the extra one in the center of the stitch. (You are actually skipping a mesh).

Work your whole design first; then put this stitch in. If you do not, you will never be able to move this stitch aside to get the others in.

**Fig. 11-5**

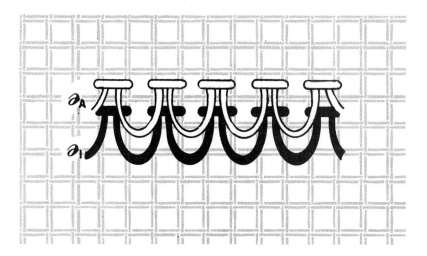

# Cut turkey work

Work just as in Looped Turkey Work, but cut the loops as you go. After working Row 2, clip Row 1; after working Row 3, clip Row 2. If you cut each row immediately after it is worked, the pieces can be easily caught in the next row as you stitch it. However, if you wait until you have completely finished the area, it is quite hard to do a good cutting job. Cut as shown in Figure b.

Cutting the loops too short causes the rows to show. See top and bottom photos for Figure 11–6.

It does not matter if you end a yarn in the middle of a row.

Persian yarn makes a fluffier Cut Turkey Work.

Work your whole design first; then put this stitch in. If you do not, you will never be able to move this stitch to get the others in.

To fluff your Turkey Work, pick at it with the point of the needle, or brush it with a stiff-bristled nylon hair brush. Trim carefully.

**Fig. 11-6**

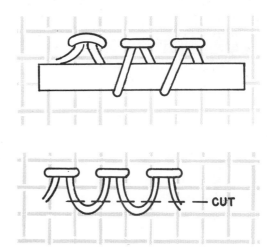

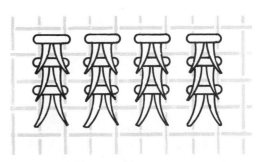

# Needleweaving

This is a kind of surface embroidery. The yarn penetrates the canvas only at the outer edges of the area covered in Needleweaving. Any pattern you wish may be woven.

**Fig. 11-7**

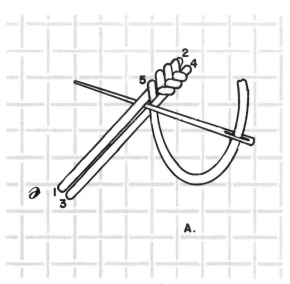

**A.**

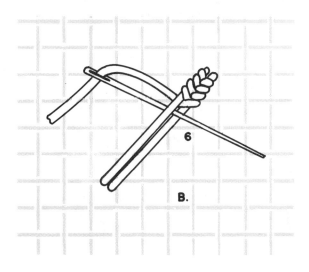

**B.**

# Running stitch

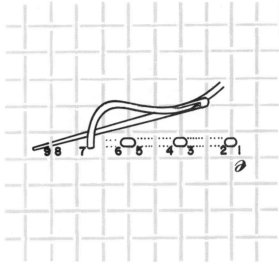

**Fig. 11-8**

# Raised buttonhole

Always work this stitch from left to right. Work the vertical rows of this stitch from top to bottom. Work the rows from left to right for a compact stitch, and work them from right to left for a lacy look.

When working the buttonhole portion of the stitch from left to right, pull the thread with your left hand, keeping it taut until the next stitch is taken. Use your fingernail or the points of small scissors to push the vertical rows together. This helps to pack the yarn in for height.

This stitch makes nice tree bark.

**Fig. 11-9**

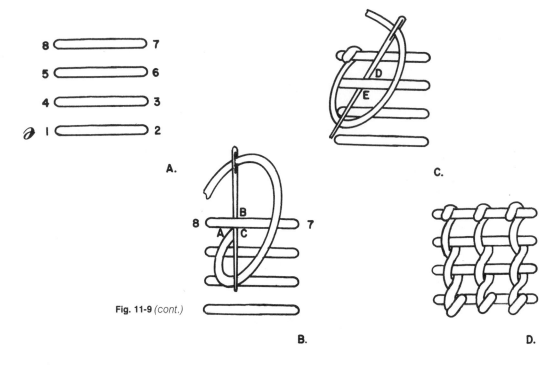

Fig. 11-9 (cont.)

A.

B.

C.

D.

## Raised buttonhole on raised band

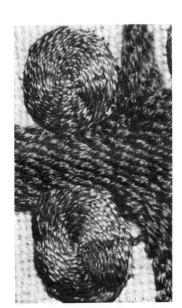

This is the same stitch as the preceding one except for the bed over which the stitch is worked. The fatter the padding you lay down, the higher the stitch will be. Lay as many stitches as you need. Build up the center for a rounded look. Stagger the start and stop of the padding stitches to get a smooth, long look. After you have laid the padding, refer to Raised Buttonhole to continue working the stitch.

This stitch is very hard to rip, so be sure that it is what you want to do before you put it in.

This stitch makes particularly nice tree bark.

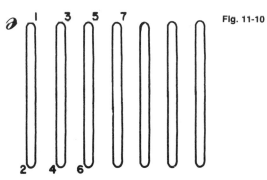

Fig. 11-10

# PART FOUR
# BLOCKING & FINISHING

*Exquisite finishing is a must. It can enhance perfect stitching and can cause sloppy stitching to be overlooked.*

*You can do this at home—just follow the directions given in the next two chapters precisely.*

*Finishing is the most critical step in doing needlepoint. It's the finishing that gives the viewer of your project that all-important first impression. Your stitching will be noticed only upon close inspection.*

*Blocking, the first step, is outlined in Chapter 12.*

*Constructing pillows, framing needlepoint, and lining needlepoint are explained in Chapter 13.*

Chapter twelve

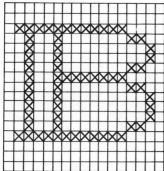

# BLOCKING

Blocking is the first step in professional finishing. Having someone else do it can cost plenty, and few peole will do it to your satisfaction, especially if you are a perfectionist!

So get busy!

## Blocking board

Needlepoint is straightened—or blocked—on a board. Insulation board works best. It is porous, so the needlepoint dries quickly. Pins and staples go into and pull out of it easily. It's cheap, too!

Buy insulation board at the lumber yard. It's known by lots of names, but they always know what you mean when you tell them it's the stuff used for bulletin boards. Sometimes, they'll give you a scrap—especially if you ask the man in the back and not the one at the counter! If you have a choice, 2′ × 2′ is a handy size.

The board must be covered. Its color rubs off easily. Its rough surface will snag your needlepoint and your clothes. Staple a brown paper bag to *both* sides of the board. Bind the edges with very wide masking tape, making sure that you cover the staples. A cheap grocery bag works better than brown wrapping paper. Don't worry if you have to piece it—it will be O.K.

Right before you go to bed, put the board in the bathtub. Wet the paper thoroughly by spraying liberally with water. *Then go to bed!* It will look so awful that you'll be sure you've done something wrong—you haven't!

The next morning, the paper will be dry, smooth, and beautifully taut!

## Making the grid

The job of blocking is a lot easier if you draw a grid of *parallel* and *perpendicular* lines on your paper. One-inch squares are nice to use, but lines the width of the yardstick are easier to make. Draw the lines with a *waterproof* marker. Test it yourself (see page 15). When the ink is completely dry, spray the board with a spray plastic (acrylic). My first one lasted about seven years and got *lots* of use!

Follow the instructions in Figure 12–1a–j.

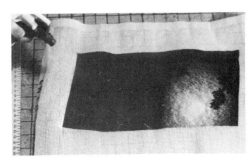

**Fig. 12-1a** *Wet your needlepoint with a spray of water.*

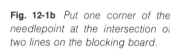

**Fig. 12-1b** *Put one corner of the needlepoint at the intersection of two lines on the blocking board.*

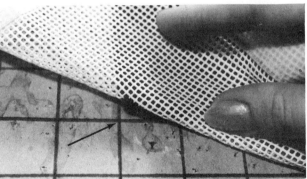

**Fig. 12-1c** *Staple this corner in place with three or four staples. They will be under lots of tension later.*

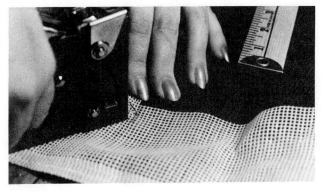

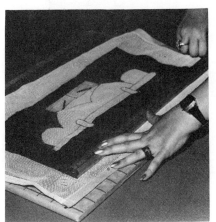

**Fig. 12-1d** *Measure along one side as shown, and staple the second corner.*

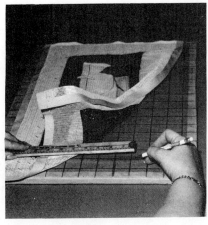

**Fig. 12-1e** *Find the point for the fourth corner by measuring. Mark this point on the blocking board.*

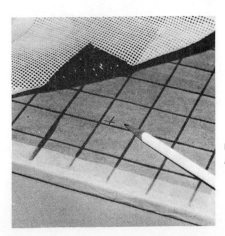

**Fig. 12-1f** *Your mark should look like this.*

**Fig. 12-1g** *Pull the fourth corner to meet your mark. If your needlepoint is badly out of shape, you'll need one to three people to help you at this point. Staple the corner in place securely.*

**Fig. 12-1h** *Is feline help better than no help at all?*

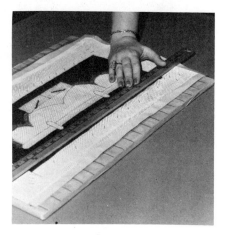

**Fig. 12-1i** *Lay a yardstick along the edge of the needlepoint to help you get the side straight.*

**Fig. 12-1j** *Staple the corners down so they'll dry flat.*

## Fastening the canvas

When you have a good margin of blank canvas around your stitching, a staple gun works well. The staples may cut a mesh or two, but if you staple well into the margin, it won't really matter. Place the staples at an angle to the mesh and about ¼" apart. This angle gives the staples a better grip on the canvas.

Pieces stitched with the Two-Step Edge-finishing Method will not have an area of blank canvas that you can staple into. Use heavy-duty *stainless steel* T-pins to block these pieces. Put the pins between the stitches and two or three stitches in from the edge—very carefully. They, too, should be ¼" apart. Blocking squashes the Binding Stitch, so do it *after* blocking.

The T-pins do leave holes in the needlepoint. Push them back together with a needle and a little steam. *NEVER ALLOW THE IRON TO TOUCH THE NEEDLEPOINT.*

Allow the needlepoint to dry *completely* before you take it off the blocking board. The drying time may be as little as 24 hours or as long as a week. If you take it off the board too soon, it will probably revert to its former crooked life. *Never* prop up the blocking board when it has wet needlepoint on it. The work may dry with a watermark on it. Watermarks *do not* come out. (How do you think I know?) Keep the board flat until the needlepoint dries. Uneven dampening also results in watermarks. (How do you think I know that, too?)

## Stains in blocking

If your yarn, paint, or marker runs during blocking, cry, but don't commit suicide! Sometimes, the stains do come out. Sponge the stain with a mixture of one teaspoon of ammonia and one cup of cold water. Rinse thoroughly.

If that doesn't work, soak the piece in cold water overnight. Sometimes the dye keeps on running—right out of your needlepoint. If soaking doesn't work, block it and let it dry. The only thing you can do now is to rip the stitches and work them again—Sorry! But always remember—Blessed is a cheerful ripper!

**HINTS**  Raised stitches can be fluffed with a shot of steam. Do *not overdo* the steam. Too much steam shrinks and mats wool—not to mention your skin!

A limp piece of needlepoint can be revived by treating the wrong side with spray starch.

Chapter thirteen

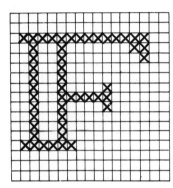INISHING

Finishing is yet another area where people think they need a professional to help. Too often, I have been charged too much for what I consider unsatisfactory finishing. Now I do it myself. And with just a little practice and a striving for perfection, you too, can achieve professional-looking results.

## Framing

Needlepoint pictures can be expensive to have finished. But if you plan ahead, you can design your project so that it fits into a standard-sized frame. There are many different styles and sizes available. Be sure to check out the sizes that are available to you *before* you cut the canvas.

Once in a while I do want a custom frame, but I still mount the needlepoint myself. That way, I'm sure it's straight.

The frame you choose should be deep enough to cover a stretcher frame, which should not show when the finished piece is properly mounted in the frame. If necessary, you can stretch your needlepoint over a piece of ¼" plywood instead of a stretcher frame. *Never* use cardboard for this job. It will buckle under the tension put on it. Cardboard also buckles with high humidity.

Never put needlepoint under glass. Wool needs to breathe.

If you learn to measure *carefully,* you will be able to fit your needlepoint into a frame of predetermined size. There should always be a 3" margin of blank canvas all the way around your design. For example, if your design area is 5" × 7", then you need to cut the canvas 11" × 13. This was figured this way: 3" + 5" + 3" = 11" and 3" + 7" + 3" = 13". See Figure 13–1a for another example.

You may think this is a lot of wasted canvas, but when it comes to blocking and framing, you'll be glad to have it. When you block, you should pull only on the blank canvas, not the stitched part. Also, framing eats up a lot of the margin.

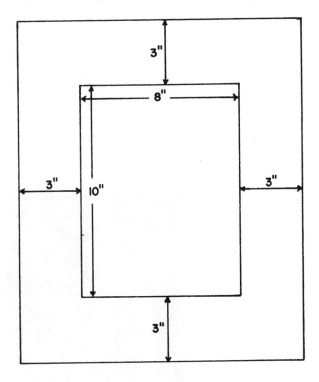

**Fig. 13-1a** *Measuring for needlepoint picture.*

A.

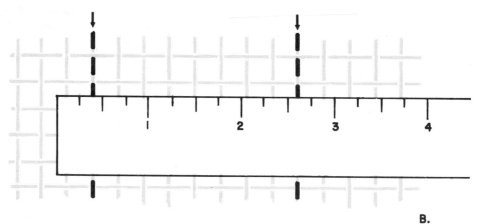

**Fig. 13-1b** *Measuring margins for a 3" picture.*

The margins should actually be 2 mesh shy (one on either side) of your measurement (see Figure 13–1b). What this really amounts to is leaving one blank mesh all the way around the design. This is your fudge factor. Mark the margins with a *waterproof* marker. Write the size of your design on the masking tape on the edge of canvas, using a waterproof marker. Use a ruler when you block, so that you can get the same measurements that you started with.

Refer to Figure 13–2a–o for instructions on framing.

**Fig. 13-2a** *Equipment needed for framing needlepoint.*

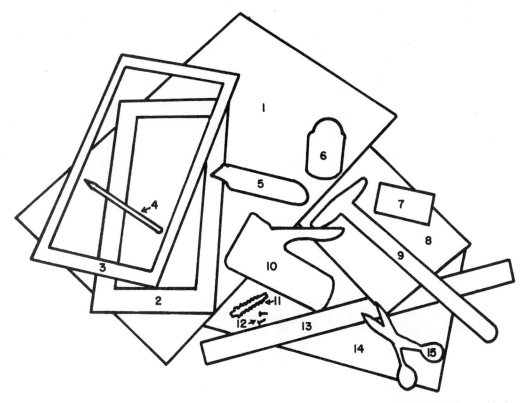

**Fig. 13-2b** *(1) tacks, (2) cardboard, (3) razor blade, (4) sawtooth hanger, (5) scissors, (6) pencil, (7) staple gun, (8) stretcher frame, (9) ruler, (10) frame, (11) square, (12) needlepoint, (13) hammer, (14) paper bag, (15) glue.*

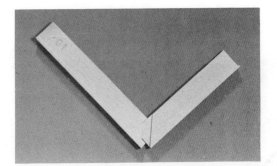

**Fig. 13-2c** *Stretcher-frame pieces fit together at the corners like this; they may need a tap of the hammer to get them all the way together.*

**Fig. 13-2d** *Use a square to be sure each is 90°.*

**Fig. 13-2e** *Try stretcher frame in frame for size; note that there is very little extra room.*

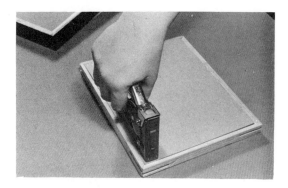

**Fig. 13-2f** *Cut a piece of cardboard a little smaller than the stretcher frame, and staple it in place on the stretcher frame; wrap the needlepoint around the stretcher frame so that the cardboard lies next to the needlepoint.*

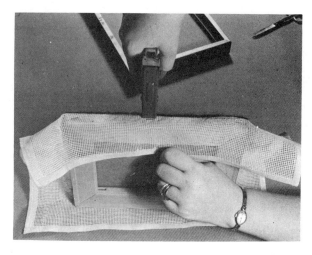

**Fig. 13-2g** *Staple the corners first, then the sides.*

**Fig. 13-2h** *When all sides are stapled, miter the corners on back; staple the middle of the piece brought to the wrong side of the stretcher frame first.*

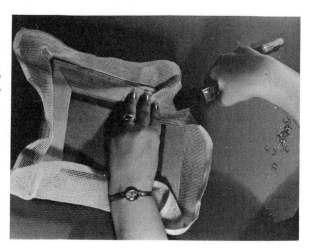

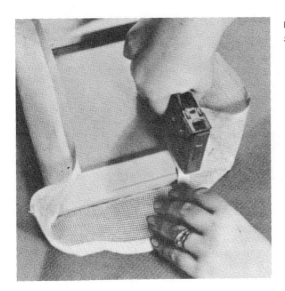

**Fig. 13-2i** *Next staple the sides of that same piece.*

**Fig. 13-2j** *Fold one side of the canvas to the back to form one-half of the mitered corner; then fold the other side back and staple; do other three corners, then staple sides between the mitered corners.*

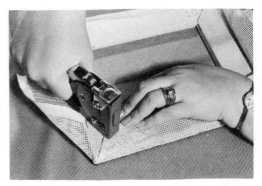

**Fig. 13-2k** *Put the stretcher frame in the frame; staple or nail the stretcher frame in place.*

**Fig. 13-2l** *Wet a piece of brown paper for the back.*

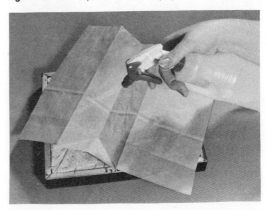

**Fig. 13-2m** *Apply Elmer's Glue-all to the back of the frame, and wipe away the excess glue with damp paper towel.*

**Fig. 13-2n** *Place paper over the back of the picture frame, and trim away excess paper with a single-edged razor blade; again wipe away excess glue.*

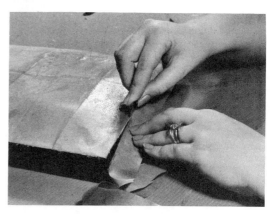

**Fig. 13-2o** *Find the center of the picture and attack a sawtooth hanger. The paper will dry out, and you will have a picture that looks better than a professional could make it.*

**Fig. 13-2p** *If you plan to wrap a piece of needlepoint around plywood or cardboard, lace sides together with heavy thread (this is a long job).*

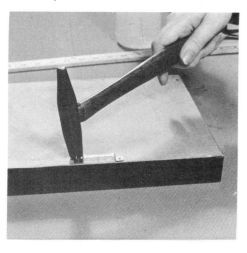

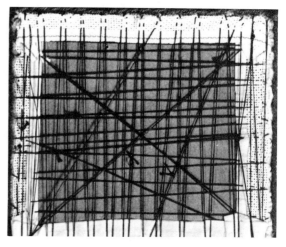

Needlepoint pillows are very popular, but they are quite expensive to have finished. If you sew, consider doing your own.

The backing fabric should be as elegant as your needlepoint. Consider synthetic suede, velvet, cotton suede cloth, or no-wale corduroy.

Place the right sides of the needlepoint and the backing fabric together and stitch as shown in Figure 13–3. Round the corners slightly.

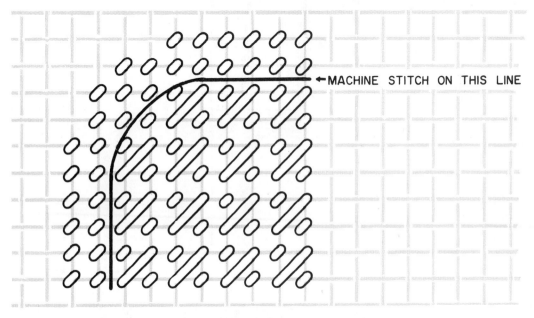

←MACHINE STITCH ON THIS LINE

**Fig. 13-3a-b** *Stitching a pillow.*

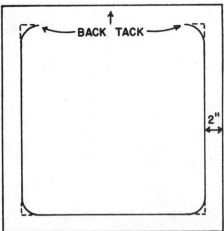

BACK TACK

2"

Trim the seams to ⅝". Zig-zag the raw edges together except at the opening; stitch those separately.

Turn and stuff with polyester fiber filling. Be sure not to forget the corners. Make the pillow plump but not fat. The sides will wrinkle if there's too much stuffing.

Pin the opening together and sew it with the Blind Stitch (see Figure 13–4). Run the needle inside the fold of the fabric. Bring it out and catch one thread of the canvas. Insert it back into the fabric again. Take stitches every ¼" to ⅜".

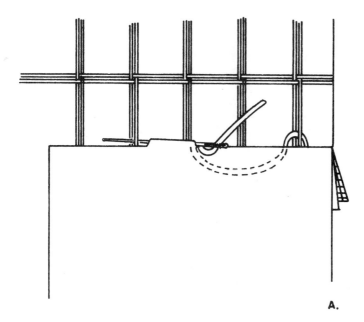

**A.**

**Fig. 13-4a-b** *Use the Blind Stitch to sew the fourth side of the pillow.*

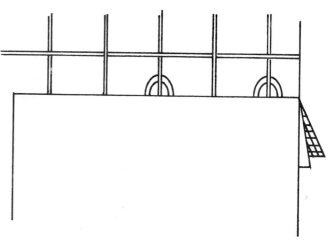

**B.**

*BLOCKING AND FINISHING*

Cording is difficult to stitch into the seam of a pillow unless you are an expert seamstress. A twisted cord is easier, and I think it's quite pretty.

It takes two people to make a twisted cord. First, measure the distance you wish to cover with the twisted cord. Multiply this number by 3. This is the amount of yarn you'll need. Let's say your pillow is 14″ × 14″. The circumference is 56″; so 56″ × 3 = 168″.

How thick your twisted cord is depends on how many strands of yarn you use. Six strands make a fine pillow cording. So, for our example, you'd need 6 strands 168″ long. Obviously, you need an uncut skein of yarn for this.

Knot the strands of yarn together at both ends and in the middle. Attach one end of the yarn to one beater of an electric mixer with a twist tie. Ask a friend to hold the other end. Keep the yarn taut. Turn the mixer on (honest!) and run it until the yarn kinks. Keeping the yarn *taut,* hook the middle knot over a hook or a third person's finger. Release the end that's on the mixer and give it to the friend who's holding the other end. Take the yarn off the hook and *slowly* release the tension. The yarn pieces will now twist together (see Figure 13–5a–d). If

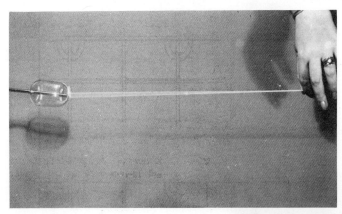

**Fig. 13-5a-d**  *Making a twisted cord.*

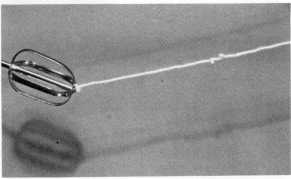

you let go too fast, the twist will be sloppy. Tie the ends together with another piece of yarn. Hand-sew the twisted cord in place. Tuck in the ends neatly.

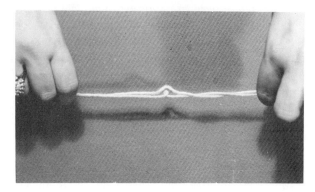

Fig. 13-5a-d *(cont.)*

## Linings

Use a lightweight fabric for lining. Turn under ⅝" for a seam allowance. Sew the lining in place with the Blind Stitch (see page 170).

If you want a padded lining, cut the fabric about ¼" bigger on all sides and stuff the lining with polyester fiber filling. Ease in the fullness.

BLOCKING AND FINISHING

# INDEX

## General index

# Stitch index